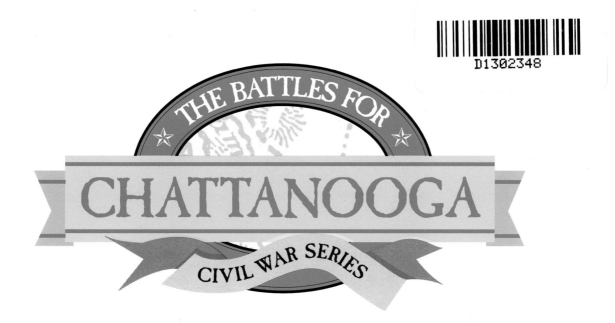

THE BATTLES FOR CHATTANOOGA

CIVIL WAR SERIES

TEXT BY PETER COZZENS

Maps by George Skoch

Thanks to James H. Ogden III at Chickamauga and Chattanooga National Military Park.

Published by Eastern National Park and Monument Association, copyright 1996.

Eastern National Park & Monument Association aids and promotes the historical, scientific, and educational activities of the National Park Service. It also supports the research, interpretation, and conservation programs of the Service. As a not-for-profit cooperating association recognized by Congress, it makes interpretive material available to park visitors and the general public.

Front cover: The Battle of Missionary Ridge by Douglas Volk, courtesy of the Minnesota Historical Society.

Back cover: The Battle of Lookout Mountain by James Walker, courtesy of U.S. Department of Defense.

THE BATTLES FOR CHATTANOOGA

The autumn of 1863 was a season of shattered hopes. In the North, the fall of Vicksburg and the turning back of Lee's invasion of Pennsylvania in July had raised expectations of an end to hostilities before Christmas. When Major General William Starke Rosecrans maneuvered General Braxton Bragg out of Tennessee that same month, victory seemed near on all fronts. But the Army of the Potomac failed to follow up its triumph at Gettysburg, and Ulysses S. Grant saw his army at Vicksburg carved up to support peripheral operations. Then in September, Rosecrans's Army of the Cumberland came to grief along the banks of Chickamauga Creek, twelve miles southeast of Chattanooga, Tennessee. In some of the bitterest fighting of the war, Bragg shattered the Union center and sent half the Federal army reeling toward Chattanooga in chaos. Only a stubborn stand by Major General George Thomas with the remainder of the army averted catastrophe. As it was, Rosecrans retired into the inner defenses of Chattanooga, too dazed to do more than await the inevitable Confederate attack.

But it never came. As Chickamauga brought a halt to the grand Federal offensives of 1863, so too did it represent a squandering of the South's last chance to turn the tide of the war in the West. Bragg had no inclination to storm Chattanooga, and the first Confederate troops did not appear on the outskirts of the city until two days after Chickamauga. Bragg was on the attack, but the object of his offensive was his own generals. At the very time his attention should have been given over to preventing the demoralized Federal army from consolidating its defenses around Chattanooga, Bragg expended his energy rousting out his detractors within the Army of Tennessee. Disgusted with Bragg's repeated failings in battle and repelled by his acerbic temperament, on October 4 twelve of his most senior generals submitted a petition to President Jefferson Davis, calling for Bragg's removal from command. Among the signatories were Lieutenant Generals James Longstreet, who had come from Virginia with his corps to take part in the Battle of Chickamauga, Daniel Harvey Hill, and Simon B. Buckner.

Davis traveled at once to the army. He listened to the complaints of Bragg's factious subordinates and to the commanding general's rebuttals. In the end, Davis sustained Bragg, who turned the

tables on the conspirators. He relieved Hill and Buckner, then reshuffled the units of their corps and that of Leonidas Polk, who had been suspended from command immediately after Chickamauga, so as to dig out the roots of the opposition.

The reconfigured army consisted of three corps. Kentuckian John C. Breckinridge commanded a corps consisting of three divisions, led by Alexander P. Stewart, William Bate, and J. Patton Anderson.

Longstreet kept his corps, less one division on loan from the Army of Tennessee that Bragg broke up, and a second that he transferred to Polk's old corps. The two remaining divisions, which Longstreet had brought with him from Virginia, were led by Brigadier General Micah Jenkins and Major General Lafayette McLaws. Between Bragg and Longstreet there could be no reconciliation. When his effort to unseat Bragg failed, Longstreet sulked. Bragg continued to hold him in high regard as a commander and entrusted him with key assignments early in the campaign, unaware that Longstreet had no inclination to obey orders.

Polk's former corps went to Lieutenant General William J. Hardee, then in Mississippi. Hardee had little to do after the fall of Vicksburg and, despite his distaste for Bragg, he was glad to return to the army.

The men in ranks shared their generals' low opinion of Bragg. "Everyone here curses Bragg," a young Tennessee lieutenant wrote home. Only Bragg's removal, he went on, would put the troops in good spirits. The dismembering of divisions and brigades eroded morale further. Desertions climbed at an alarming rate: 2,149 for the months of September and October alone.

More than just bad generalship drove the Rebels to desert. Rations were short and shelter scarce, hardships the men could more readily have endured had they felt Bragg had some strategy in mind beyond waiting for the Federals to starve first. But, a Virginian bemoaned in early October, "Bragg is so much afraid of doing something which would look like taking advantage of an enemy that he does nothing. He would not strike Rosecrans another blow until he has recovered his strength and announces himself ready. Our great victory of [Chickamauga] has been turned to ashes."

But there was little chance of Rosecrans recovering his strength. Chickamauga had wrecked him. His strategic thinking was fuzzy, and he lacked the strength to sustain a coherent effort to relieve his beleaguered army.

Certainly the task before Rosecrans was daunting enough to give any commander pause. Few cities were both so vulnerable to siege or offered topographical features so favorable to the defense as Chattanooga. Natural obstacles of imposing grandeur encircled it. If protected, they might keep a besieging army at bay

. . . there was little chance of Rosecrans recovering his strength. Chickamauga had wrecked him. His strategic thinking was fuzzy, and he lacked the strength to sustain a coherent effort to relieve his beleaguered army.

indefinitely, but Rosecrans had lost them to Bragg without firing a shot in their defense, so the Federals found themselves ensnared between a wide river and a series of long ridges and craggy bluffs.

Chattanooga lay in a bend of the Tennessee River, which turned abruptly to the south just beyond the city, continuing in that direction for two miles before butting up against Lookout Mountain. A half-mile beyond the base of Lookout Mountain, the river veered nearly due north. It flowed north for two miles before forking at Williams Island. These two major changes of the river's course after Chattanooga—first to the south, then back to the north—created a long, narrow peninsula opposite Lookout Mountain that was called Moccasin Point.

From many miles northeast of Chattanooga to the southern tip of Williams Island, the Tennessee River held

steady at a width of three to five hundred yards, its current gentle and waters placid. Where the two branches reunited north of the island, the river turned narrow and rapid. After thirteen miles of dizzying twists and foaming water, the river calmed and widened near Kelley's Ferry, which lay six miles west of the northern tip of Lookout Mountain. From Kelley's Ferry, the Tennessee was easily navigable all the way to the Federal supply depot at Bridgeport, Alabama, twenty-two miles away.

The ground east of Chattanooga was nearly as formidable a barrier as the river. Two miles beyond the town, rising from a broad and partly cleared valley to a height of nearly five hundred feet, loomed Missionary Ridge.

Missionary Ridge grew out of the southern bank of South Chickamauga Creek, which emptied into the Tennessee River two and a half miles northeast of the city. Bisected by wagon roads, broken by ravines, dotted with huge outcroppings, and tangled with fallen timber, Missionary Ridge ran south by slightly southeast for nearly fifteen miles. Hard to ascend along its entire length, its slopes were particularly precipitous along the eight-mile stretch from South Chickamauga Creek to Rossville, Georgia, where a narrow gap sliced through the ridge.

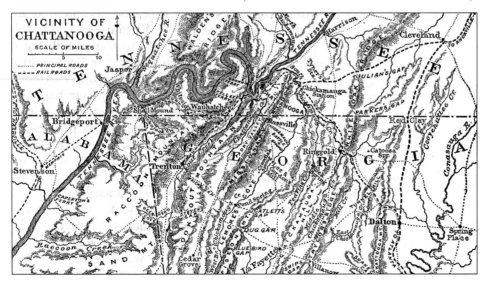

VICINITY OF
CHATTANOOGA
SCALE OF MILES

Missionary Ridge was separated from its more spectacular sister elevation to the west, Lookout Mountain, by the four-mile-wide Chattanooga Creek, which flowed north, then curved west to empty into the Tennessee River at the base of Lookout.

Lookout Mountain was not a single mountain in the commonly understood sense but a long, towering ridge that extended southward from the Tennessee river eighty-five miles. Lookout Mountain narrowed as it neared the river, coming to a point two hundred yards wide and eighteen hundred feet above the Tennessee.

From the riverbank, the mountain first rose at a forty-five-degree angle. About two-thirds of the way between the river and the summit, the slope rose sharply, then changed grade and became relatively level before terminating in a ledge, or "bench," between 150 and 300 feet wide, which extended for several miles around both sides of the mountain.

From the bench, the grade again became steep. Five hundred feet of timber and outcrops brought one to the "palisades," which a war correspondent described as "a ridge of dark, cold, gray rocks, bare even of moss, which rise to the height of fifty or sixty feet."

West of Lookout Mountain loomed Sand Mountain. A long valley of varying width and names divided Sand from Lookout Mountain. Of similar length, Sand Mountain was cut by the mile-wide Running Water Creek Valley five miles south of the Tennessee River. The mountain resumed north of the valley, and this final stretch was called Raccoon Mountain. It lay two miles west of Lookout Mountain. Near the river, the plain separating the two ranges was known as Lookout Valley. A narrow stream called Lookout Creek ran along the western side of Lookout Mountain and emptied into the Tennessee north of the point of the mountain. On either side of the valley, a chain of foothills rubbed against the two mountains.

Of course, this mosaic of natural obstacles rendered lines of supply and communications into Chattanooga from the north and west extremely vulnerable. Confederate depredations and Bragg's tightening noose around Chattanooga forced Rosecrans to use the longest and

most indirect route, an excruciating course through the mountains nearly sixty miles in length, to bring supplies from Bridgeport, Alabama, into the city.

As September drew to a close, heavy rains began to fall. Roads were beaten to paste, and in the mountains, long stretches were washed away. The Confederates made common cause with nature. On October 1, Major General Joseph Wheeler's cavalry descended on an eight-hundred-wagon train rumbling over Walden's Ridge, burning the wagons and shooting the mules.

Wheeler's raid was "the funeral pyre of Rosecrans in top command." Three Federal divisions were left without supplies, and the ammunition reserves of the entire army were rendered dangerously low. By mid-October, the Army of the Cumberland was on the brink of starvation.

An unparalleled opportunity had been presented to Bragg, but he was too absorbed in his internecine struggles to fashion a coherent plan for compelling the Federals to abandon Chattanooga.

WHEELER'S CONFEDERATE CAVALRY CAPTURE A SUPPLY TRAIN. ILLUSTRATION BY J. T. E. HILLEN.

(NY PUBLIC LIBRARY PRINT COLLECTION)

Bragg's actions against the Federal army at Chattanooga during October were little better than a series of poorly thought out, makeshift measures conceived during the odd moments between battles with his generals.

His troop dispositions offered little possibility of anything more. A direct assault was out of the question. Bragg had a mere forty-six thousand infantrymen stretched out along a seven-mile front that ran from the foot of Lookout Mountain to Missionary Ridge and then northward along the base of the ridge to a point a half-mile south of the Chattanooga and Cleveland Railroad. Bragg lacked even the troops needed to extend the line to the Tennessee River, which was the only way truly to hem in the Federals. Instead, Bragg shook out a thin picket line up the riverbank as far as the mouth of South Chickamauga Creek to guard against crossings beyond his right flank. Longstreet's corps held the line from the base of Lookout Mountain to the west bank of Chattanooga Creek; Breckinridge occupied the center from the east bank to the Bird's Mill road across Missionary Ridge, and Polk's old corps—temporarily commanded by Benjamin Franklin Cheatham—completed the line along the foot of the ridge. Tucked behind a chain of earthen redoubts and rifle pits, the Federals were a mile or more beyond the attenuated Rebel main line in most places. Their lines, by contrast, were neatly compact. Extending from bank to bank of the

Tennessee, they formed a half-circle around Chattanooga three miles long. Opposing pickets were often less than two hundred yards apart, placed so as to give ample warning of an advance by either side.

Not that anyone was about to move. Rosecrans had neither the will nor the horses needed to move his army. And Bragg spent his time sulking about headquarters reading, with little interest, ciphered messages warning of the approach of five Yankee divisions under Major General William T. Sherman from Mississippi.

Victory at Vicksburg had been barren for Major General Ulysses S. Grant. After the city's fall in July 1862, General in Chief Henry Halleck began carving up Grant's army to enable Union forces west of the Mississippi to "clean up a little in the weaker Trans-Mississippi Department before undertaking anything ambitious against the stronger half of the Confederacy." Only the defeat of the Army of the Cumberland at Chickamauga and its retreat to Chattanooga saved Grant from being shunted aside by Halleck, who was always jealous of Grant's successes. On September 29, six days after Halleck ordered Grant to send William T. Sherman to Chattanooga, Secretary of War Edwin Stanton directed Grant to go to Chattanooga himself as commander of the newly created Military Division of the Mississippi, an enormous field command that was to be composed of three depart-

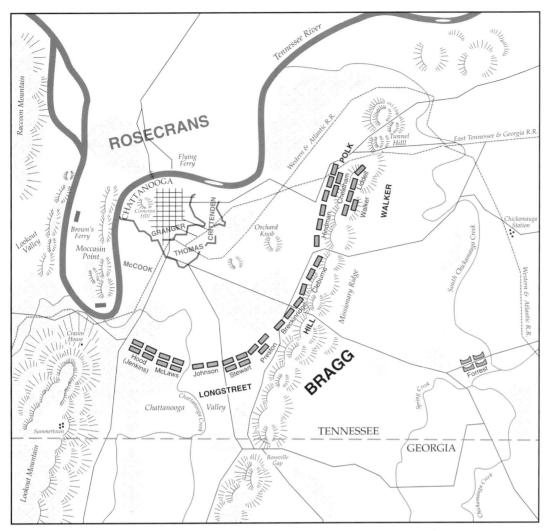

BRAGG LAYS SIEGE TO CHATTANOOGA, SEPTEMBER 24, 1863
Rosecrans has withdrawn the Army of the Cumberland into Chattanooga. Houses, buildings, and trees on the edge of the city were removed for construction material and to create fields of fire. Federal forces stationed on Moccasin Point guarded the approaches into the city from Lookout Mountain and Lookout Valley.

Bragg deployed the Army of Tennessee in positions along the base of Missionary Ridge, across Chattanooga Valley, and to the northern toe of Lookout Mountain. Longstreet's forces soon occupied Lookout Mountain and extended a small number of troops into Lookout Valley closing off all the Federal supply routes into Chattanooga but the northern one.

ments: the Department of the Ohio, then under Major General Ambrose Burnside; the Department of the Cumberland, under Rosecrans; and Grant's own Department of the Tennessee. In effect, all the territory from the Appalachians to the Mississippi River and including much of the state of Arkansas was to be unified under one commander. Grant was given the option of retaining or dismissing Rosecrans; he chose to replace Rosecrans with his senior corps commander, Major General George H. Thomas.

Grant arrived at Chattanooga on October 23. General Thomas was ready with a formal briefing. He made a few general remarks, then gave the floor over to Major General William Farrar "Baldy" Smith, a recent arrival to the Army of the Cumberland whom Rosecrans had made

GENERAL ROSECRANS (SEATED FOURTH FROM LEFT) AND STAFF.

(THE WESTERN RESERVE HISTORICAL SOCIETY)

chief engineer of the Department of the Cumberland. Before being relieved, Rosecrans had devised a plan for reopening the river supply route to Bridgeport, which would dramatically cut both the time and risk to Union supply efforts. Fundamental to Rosecrans's plan was the conviction that General Joseph Hooker must move from Bridgeport with his force from the Army of the Potomac to occupy Lookout Valley and seize the passes of Lookout Mountain before a bridge could be thrown across the Tennessee River from Moccasin Point, for the last leg of the journey into Chattanooga.

Reconnoitering possible bridge sites the week before, Smith had come upon a spot on the western side of Moccasin Point known locally as Brown's Ferry that struck him as ideal. Its tactical importance was obvious. The only road along that stretch of the river cut through a gap in a chain of foothills that lined the shore opposite Brown's Ferry. More significant, less than a quarter mile beyond the gap the road turned south and became the primary wagon road through Lookout Valley as far south as Wauhatchie, where it forked, meeting a road that ran west all the way to Kelley's Ferry. The gap itself struck Smith as an ideal crossing site. Narrow but deep, it split the foothills just

above the level of the river. Only a few Rebel picket posts were in evidence.

Smith stood before a large map of the region and spoke passionately of his plan to Grant. Grant was impressed. He approved Smith's scheme for opening the supply route now known as the cracker line and delegated its execution to Thomas and Smith.

The two worked quickly. Thomas immediately wired Hooker detailed marching orders. He was to detach Major General Henry Slocum with one division of the Twelfth Corps to guard the rail line from Murfreesboro to Bridgeport. With the remaining division, under Brigadier General John Geary, and Howard's Eleventh Corps, Hooker was to cross the Tennessee River at Bridgeport and move as rapidly as possible to Lookout Valley.

Hooker was slow in starting. His command was scattered across the countryside north of Bridgeport. With the roads still miserable quagmires from the rains, it would be a day, perhaps two, before he would be ready to move.

Grant was annoyed but not alarmed. He no longer shared Smith's conviction that Hooker's thrust into Lookout Valley must occur simultaneously. As he now saw things, the capture of Brown's Ferry and the hills flanking it would permit him to forestall the sort of Rebel concentration in Lookout Valley designed to drive back Hooker that Smith feared. A lodgment at Brown's Ferry would enable Grant to throw a force against the right flank of any Rebel units that ventured into the valley.

As Thomas kept an eye on Hooker's progress, Smith set about organizing the

assault on Brown's Ferry. One brigade would travel downriver under the cover of darkness from Chattanooga to Brown's Ferry; there the troops were to disembark and capture the gorge and hills on the west bank. The hazards were clear: the men would be floating targets for nine miles. Rebel batteries atop Lookout might reduce the flotilla to splinters. Smith judged the reward worth the risk.

Meanwhile, a second brigade and the artillery were to march across Moccasin Point to the ferry in time to cross the river in support of the assaulting force.

Smith chose his brigade wisely. For the river-borne force he selected the command of Brigadier General William Hazen, a proven fighter whose daring was exceeded only by his ambition. To lead the supporting brigade, Smith called on the "Mad Russian," Brigadier General John Turchin.

No one at Bragg's headquarters atop Missionary Ridge had an inkling of what was about to unfold over in Lookout Valley. And they were not going to find out, if matters were left to General Longstreet. Bragg had accurate information on Sherman's progress across northern Mississippi, thanks to Stephen Dill Lee's cavalry. Closer to home, he learned from scouts on October 25 that Hooker was preparing to cross the river at Bridgeport. That same day, Major James Austin's Ninth Kentucky Cavalry came upon Yankee engineers rebuilding the railroad trestles in the gorge of Running Water Creek.

Austin's report worried Bragg. He ordered Longstreet to make a close reconnaissance toward Bridgeport and to protect his left flank, presumably by moving additional units into Lookout Valley.

Nothing happened; Longstreet simply laid aside Bragg's instructions. Still smarting over President Davis's decision to retain Bragg, Longstreet probably reasoned that, if he could not command the

army, he might at least run his corps as he saw fit.

In truth, Longstreet was doing a poor job at even that. After committing Evander Law's brigade to the defense of Lookout Valley in early October, Longstreet gave no further thought to that all-important avenue of approach.

Matters there were worse than Bragg could have imagined. Law went on a leave of absence. For reasons known only to himself, Brigadier General Micah Jenkins recalled Law's three reserve regiments to the east side of Lookout Mountain on October 25, leaving only Colonel William Oates with the Fifteenth Alabama near Brown's Ferry and the Fourth Alabama scattered northward along the bank of the river.

Shortly after midnight on October 26, the soldiers of Hazen's brigade were assembled at the embarkation point. The moon sank below the horizon. A heavy

GENERAL
BRAXTON BRAGG

(USAMHI)

HAZEN'S MEN FLOAT
DOWN THE TENNESSEE
RIVER NEAR
BROWN'S FERRY.

(NPS)

mist rolled into the valley, blanketing the river. Only then did company officers learn of their destination.

All was ready at 3:00 A.M. on October 27. The boats glided past the

looming point of Lookout Mountain. At 4:30 A.M. the lead flatboat thudded against the riverbank at Brown's Ferry. Ten minutes after the last pontoon landed, Brown's Ferry was in Federal hands. Out in the valley beyond the ferry, Colonel Oates was shaken awake as the first light of dawn touched the hilltops. A frightened private from the scattered picket force told him of the Yankee crossing.

The cracking of axes against trees told Oates where to find the Federals, but in the dark he could not guess their numbers. He attacked nonetheless, and his Alabamians were slaughtered. Oates himself fell with a bullet through the arm. Carried to a house near the mouth of Lookout Creek, Oates met General Law at the head of his three reserve regiments. "I told him that he was too late, in my opinion, to accomplish anything; that a heavy force had already crossed the river," recalled Oates. Thoroughly disgusted, Law placed his brigade astride the road over Lookout Mountain and reported the disaster to Longstreet.

Brown's Ferry was a scant three miles from Longstreet's headquarters. But it may as well have been in another country, for all the attention Longstreet paid it. Moccasin Point and Lookout Mountain not only blocked the general's view of the ferry but also blinded him to its tactical significance. He greeted Law's frantic dispatch announcing the fall of Brown's Ferry with an indifference that amounted to dereliction of duty. Confident that the Yankee crossing was merely a feint to cover a Federal approach along the length of Lookout Mountain, beginning near Trenton, Longstreet tucked away Law's message and gave the matter no further thought; nor did he bother to inform Bragg of what had happened. Longstreet's odd notion of a Federal threat from the south was the product of his imagination. He had neglected to reconnoiter toward Bridgeport as Bragg ordered, nor did he have scouts out in the direction of Trenton to test his assumption.

Up on Missionary Ridge, Bragg exploded with rage when he learned that Brown's Ferry had fallen. He rued ever having given Longstreet so much responsibility and sent word to him to retake the lost ground at once.

Again Longstreet did nothing. He let the day slip away and permitted Smith's Federals to consolidate their bridgehead unmolested. He argued with Bragg well into the night of October 27 that the enemy was moving on Trenton in force. Bragg was unconvinced. To prevent further misunderstanding, Bragg met Longstreet atop Lookout Mountain the next morning. Their discussion was cut short by a startling discovery: a long and powerful Federal column had emerged from the gorge of Running Water Creek and was marching down Lookout Valley. Fourteen hundred feet below and less than a mile west from where Bragg and Longstreet stood was the head of Hooker's column, closing on the valley hamlet of Wauhatchie.

Hooker made good time down the valley, reaching Brown's Ferry at 3:45 P.M. The joy of Hazen's and Turchin's men, on seeing the easterners' approach, "was beyond description," said an officer in Hazen's brigade.

With the wagon road to Bridgeport

open and the river clear to Kelley's Ferry, Thomas and his staff worked late into the night to see to it that rations would begin to flow over the Cracker Line into Chattanooga. Difficulties remained, but Thomas felt confident enough to wire Halleck that night that he hoped "in a few days to be pretty well supplied."

Of course, that was contingent upon Hooker and Smith holding open the wagon road across the northern stretch of Lookout Valley, which linked Brown's Ferry with Kelley's Ferry. For the master of Brown's Ferry, that should have been an easy task, but Smith was deeply troubled. Hooker had not taken up any military position but directed the commanders to find good cover for the troops and encamp for the night. The divisions of Adolph von Steinwehr and Carl Schurz bivouacked haphazardly in the fields on either side of the road, a half-mile above Brown's Ferry.

Hooker's most egregious error was his placement of John Geary's tiny division, down to just 1,500 men, at Wauhatchie. There were two viable approaches across the valley to Kelley's Ferry, one the wagon road over the northern base of Lookout Mountain near the river, the other a country lane that left the valley road at Wauhatchie and wound its way northwest toward a gorge in Raccoon Mountain that ended at the ferry. Hooker was confident that Howard could intercept any force attempting to move against Kelley's Ferry by way of the northern approach but worried that the Rebels might use the road from Wauhatchie if it were left undefended. Consequently, he ordered Geary to halt there for the night.

Geary obeyed the order with grave misgivings. He saw the danger of his exposed position under the heights of Lookout, from which the Confederates could watch his every move. As night fell and a brilliant, nearly full moon rose over Lookout Valley, Geary ordered his two brigade commanders, Brigade General

George Sears Greene and Colonel George A. Cobham, Jr., to bivouac their commands upon their arms. With the infantry were four guns of Knap's Pennsylvania battery, one section of which was led by Geary's son, Lieutenant Edward Geary.

The men camped along the northern fringe of a forest 300 yards north of where the Trenton Railroad joined the Nashville and Chattanooga line. A broad corn field lay beyond the forest. On the southern edge of the field stood a log cabin belonging to the Rowden family. Northeast of the cabin was a low knoll. The railroad tracks, which ran upon an embankment, skirted the knoll. Fifty yards south of the cabin rose another knoll; atop it Geary planted Knap's battery. The country lane to Kelley's Ferry marked the northern limit of the Rowden Field, and a swamp bordered it on the west.

Geary spread his picket posts so as to encircle the division bivouac, pushing sentinels as far as Lookout Creek, and waited.

There had been no meeting of the minds between Bragg and Longstreet during their morning encounter atop Lookout Mountain. Watching Hooker move down the valley, Bragg demanded that Longstreet attack Brown's Ferry, even though it would mean taking on two more Yankee divisions. Longstreet begged leave to attack by moonlight that night. Bragg agreed.

No sooner had Bragg left than Longstreet lost interest in the attack. He failed to tell Law, whose brigade, being nearest the enemy, would play a leading role in any assault, that he should prepare for action at dusk. Longstreet probably would have ignored Bragg's order, had it not been for Hooker's cavalier deployment of Geary's division. Loitering about

Sunset Rock in the waning of the late autumn afternoon, Longstreet was startled to see what he assessed to be the Yankee rear guard, burdened with a large wagon train, stop and bivouac "immediately in front of the point upon which we stood."

Longstreet conceived a plan of his own. He would indeed attack: not the Federal main body at Brown's Ferry, as Bragg had demanded, but the isolated force at Wauhatchie. He told Micah Jenkins to bring his remaining brigades over Lookout Mountain as soon as it was dark. Pleased at the prospect of offensive action of any sort, Bragg consented to Longstreet's plan.

Longstreet's planning was erratic—he failed to give either Jenkins or Law clear orders—and his choice of units to carry out the operation was foolish. Between Jenkins and Law there existed a nasty rivalry that had started when Jenkins was given permanent command of Hood's division over Law after Chickamauga.

The two brigadier generals met shortly after nightfall. Jenkins briefed Law on what was expected of him. With his own brigade, commanded by Colonel James Sheffield, and that of Brigadier General James Robertson, Law was to hold the high ground east of the Brown's Ferry road and slash at the flank of any Yankee column that might venture south to relieve the force at Wauhatchie, which Jenkins would attack with his brigade under Colonel John Bratton. Brigadier General Henry Benning's Georgia Brigade was to be held on Law's left, to reinforce Bratton as needed.

Law formed his line of battle on the designated hill and began to fortify it. At 10:00 P.M., Robertson reported with his brigade. Law told him to hold his command in a field behind the hill, both to act as a reserve and to watch the gap that existed between Law's right and the river.

It was nearly midnight before Bratton crossed Lookout Creek. Long, dark clouds rolled over the valley, blanketing the moon and cutting visibility to less than one hundred yards. Bratton's South Carolinians stepped off gaily, believing that they were going out to capture a lightly guarded wagon train. A few minutes after midnight, Bratton's skirmishers collided with Geary's pickets near the creek, overrunning the outpost and driving south along the Brown's Ferry road.

In Geary's camp, bedlam reigned. "The night was still and chilly and the men, roused suddenly from coveted sleep, were dazed and trembled from chilliness and the nervous strain induced by the unexpected situation," said a New Yorker. "They were thoroughly surprised and unprepared for an enemy whose presence they could not divine."

Geary's division deployed in a "V," with the base pointing north. Both sides fought with a brutal tenacity, the blackness of the night feeding their fear. Colonel Bratton tried to maneuver his brigade so as to outflank his numerically equal foe. He also spread his command out in a "V," which opened toward the Federals.

Three of Bratton's regiments hit Geary's line head-on. They came within a stone's throw of the Federal ranks before grinding to a halt on the north side of the Rowden field. Frustrated in their advance, the South Carolinians took aim at the gunners and horses of Knap's battery, atop the knoll only 200 yards away.

Their aim was good. Lieutenant Geary bent down to sight a cannon. He stood up again, yelled "Fire," then fell dead with a bullet between the eyes. Twenty-two of forty-eight artillerymen were shot down, along with thirty-seven of their forty-eight horses.

Although Bratton made no headway against Geary's flanks, he gave no thought to breaking off the attack. He reported, "The enemy line of fire at this time was not more than 300 to 400 yards in length . . . the sparkling fire making a splendid pyrotechnic display."

And by 3:00 A.M., that fire was weakening. Fumbling for their last cartridges, the men on the line prepared for the worst. "It looked as if the engagement would end in a hand-to-hand struggle," speculated a Pennsylvanian.

He was wrong. At the instant his confidence surged to an apex, Bratton was handed a note from Jenkins ordering him to withdraw. A strong Yankee column was pushing up the valley two miles in his rear, the message warned. It had

GEARY'S FEDERAL TROOPS HOLD THEIR GROUND AGAINST THE CONFEDERATE ATTACK AT WAUHATCHIE IN THIS PAINTING BY WILLIAM TRAVIS.

(SMITHSONIAN INSTITUTION)

THIS HOUSE IN CHATTANOOGA SERVED AS THOMAS'S HEADQUARTERS.

(LC)

likelihood that the Rebels also were trying to wedge their way between his relieving column and Brown's Ferry. Believing it imperative that Law's hill be secured, Hooker abandoned his resolve to assist Geary with his entire command and ordered an attack on the hill. Under a mistaken impression that Schurz was leading the march (he actually had fallen behind Steinwehr) and thus well on his way to Geary, Hooker threw Orland Smith's brigade of Steinwehr's division into the assault. When Law repelled Smith handily, Hooker and his lieutenants were thrown into a frenzy. Troop commanders pushed on or hesitated, according to their natures. Bewildered staff officers, separated from their superiors, issued orders recklessly. The valley road and fields to the west thronged with troops moving about without a purpose. Only Tyndale's brigade, with Carl Schurz leading it, kept on toward Wauhatchie—one brigade of the original two divisions Hooker had dispatched to Geary.

Soon even that force was distracted from its purpose. Coming up opposite the first rise south of Law's hill, Schurz was

engaged Law and now threatened to cut off Bratton from the bridge over Lookout Creek. Bratton stuffed the note in his pocket and recalled his troops.

The Federal column consisted of Hooker's tired easterners, awakened by the first volleys from Bratton's advance against Geary. Startled by the firing, Hooker was in mortal terror that his disregard for Geary's exposed position might cost him the division, and he told Carl Schurz to "double-quick" his men to Wauhatchie. Unexpected opposition from Law's brigade as the Federals marched past its position forced them to halt and deploy at 2:30 A.M. Geary already had been fighting for two hours.

Convinced that Geary was nearly annihilated, Hooker now confronted the

told by an officer from Hooker's staff to take it. Schurz questioned the wisdom of the order but halted and deployed Tyndale. At this point, General Howard ceased to be a player in the dark comedy. Perhaps feeling superfluous, he begged Hooker to allow him to continue on his own. Hooker agreed, and Howard rode off with his cavalry escort.

The only officer above the rank of regimental commander who kept his head was Colonel Smith, who charged the hill again, despite being badly outnumbered. Smith's second assault certainly would have failed had Law not then given up the contest as lost. Staff officers reported that Bratton had been repelled and was falling back over Lookout Creek. Concluding that a further sacrifice of lives would be useless, Law withdrew from the hill just as Smith's men lurched toward his works.

The carrying of the hill did little to settle Hooker's nerves. It was 4:30 A.M., and the firing from Wauhatchie had died away. Hooker told Schurz to hurry on to Geary's camp—on the assumption it still existed.

General Howard and his escort entered Geary's lines at 4:00 A.M. Geary had lost 216 men, including his son. Bratton lost 356. It had been a senseless affair. Hooker had left Geary exposed in the valley and invited an attack to no good end; Grant was disgusted and of a mind to relieve Hooker. Longstreet had accepted Howard's challenge with a force far too small to offer a reasonable chance of success.

Only the Federals had anything to be thankful for. As General Howard wrote his wife: "God has been good and sparing and given us the victory and we have opened the river from Bridgeport almost to Chattanooga." Grant too would con-

cede as much. "The cracker line" was opened, he later wrote, and "never afterward disturbed."

Bragg was less charitable with troublesome subordinates than Grant. After the Wauhatchie fiasco, he looked about for a means to rid himself of Longstreet.

President Davis provided it. Two days earlier, he had reminded Bragg that "the period most favorable for actual operations is rapidly passing away." He suggested that Bragg send Longstreet with his two divisions into East Tennessee to clear out Ambrose Burnside, who had occupied Knoxville in September. That done, Longstreet would be well situated to return to Virginia, where Robert E. Lee was reminding Davis of his urgent need for Longstreet and his 15,000 troops. Davis's suggestion that Bragg detach

FEDERAL TROOPS CAMPED INSIDE CHATTANOOGA AFTER THE BATTLE.

(WESTERN RESERVE HISTORICAL SOCIETY)

Longstreet reflected both his lack of appreciation of the gravity of the Union buildup at Chattanooga and the degree to which he was swayed by Robert E. Lee. Bragg was in a position to know better, but he was beyond the force of logical persuasion. On November 3, he called his corps commanders to a council of war. Longstreet had heard rumors that he was to be sent away, but he was unprepared for the finality of Bragg's decision. Bragg told him to move out

immediately "to drive Burnside out of East Tennessee first, or better, to capture or destroy him" and to repair the railroad. Along the way, he would be joined by most of the army's cavalry. Bragg would order the divisions of Carter Stevenson and Benjamin Franklin Cheatham, which had been sent into East Tennessee on Burnside's flank, to return to Chattanooga at once, making a net loss to the army of about 4,000 infantry and nearly all of its remaining cavalry.

Few were sorry to see Longstreet go. All but Bragg, however, seemed troubled by any diminution of the army before the Federal buildup at Chattanooga and by the wild reshuffling of forces along the line that Longstreet's departure would necessitate. Bragg's determination to hold the Chattanooga front at all, now that Lookout Valley had been lost, struck most as foolhardy.

They were right. Bragg had committed the most egregious error of his checkered career. Without a coherent plan, he divided his army in the face of a now numerically superior foe who was about to receive even more reinforcements.

Grant passed the days following Wauhatchie more productively than did his harrowed opponent. "Having got the Army of the Cumberland in a comfortable position, I now began to look after the remainder of my new command." Unremitting pressure from Washington "to do something for Burnside's relief" and his own lack of confidence in Burnside led him to turn his attention to East Tennessee. Although many of his problems were creations of his own mind, Burnside did face considerable obstacles, as Grant readily conceded.

Grant was at a loss how to respond. Thomas's soldiers were too fagged from prolonged hunger to endure a sustained offensive. And, recalled Grant, "We had not at Chattanooga animals to pull a single piece of artillery, much less a supply train. Reinforcements could not help Burnside, because he had neither supplies nor ammunition sufficient for them; hardly, indeed, bread and meat for the men he had. There was no relief possible for him except by expelling the enemy from Missionary Ridge and about Chattanooga." And this he was in no position to do.

"Nothing was left to be done but to answer Washington dispatches as best I could; urge Sherman forward . . . and encourage Burnside to hold on."

In truth, Sherman needed little urging during his march across northern Mississippi and Alabama. He moved with commendable swiftness until the head of his column reached Fayetteville, Tennessee, on November 8. There, his command ran up against an extension of the Cumberland Mountains. It was seventy miles between the Army of the Tennessee and Stevenson, Alabama, as the crow flies —nearly one hundred should Sherman choose to follow the line of the railroad, which began at Fayetteville, turned east to Winchester, and then ran south to Stevenson.

Sherman elected to follow the latter route. Even so, his army confronted obstacles similar to those that had wrecked countless wagon trains of the Army of the Cumberland along Walden's Ridge. Five days were lost covering the sixty miles between Fayetteville and Winchester. Beyond Winchester the route was a series of precipitous ascents and dizzying declines. Then, on November 14, the rains returned—hard and cold.

As steadily as the rain came telegrams from Washington, exhorting Grant to action. Grant shared his concern with his friend Sherman: "The enemy have moved a great part of their force from this point toward Burnside. I am anxious to see your old corps here at the earliest moment." On November 13, after Sherman's command arrived at Bridgeport, Grant urged him to hurry ahead to Chattanooga by himself. Sherman boarded a steamboat bound for Kelley's Ferry that night.

Grant had plenty of time on his hands during the two weeks between the Wauhatchie fight and Sherman's arrival at Bridgeport. He turned over to Smith and Thomas responsibility for developing the details of the plan that would place Sherman's army in a position to attack Bragg's right flank on the north end of Missionary Ridge. But he made it clear that no plan would be adopted until Sherman approved it.

Skeptical of the scheme, Thomas conceded the initiative to Smith, who seized it with his usual vigor. Beginning on November 8, he made daily rides north of Chattanooga, reconnoitering the ground from Brown's Ferry to the knoll opposite the mouth of South Chickamauga Creek.

Smith's analysis of the terrain revealed two critical facts. First, although the enemy on Lookout Mountain would have a clear view of Sherman's army when it crossed the bridge at Brown's Ferry, the column would disappear from sight after it passed Moccasin Point and entered the foothills along the north bank of the river opposite Chattanooga. As Grant put it, the Rebels "would be at a loss to know whether they were moving to Knoxville or held on the north side of the river for future operations at Chattanooga." Second, Smith's study showed that the northern end of Missionary Ridge was lightly defended. Only a handful of cavalry pickets patrolled the Confederate side of the river from the mouth of South Chickamauga Creek to the right flank of Bragg's army.

By the morning of November 14, the general plan of battle had taken shape.

A PHOTOGRAPH OF GRANT CIRCA 1863.

(CHICAGO HISTORICAL SOCIETY)

Subject to Sherman's blessing, it stood as follows: Roads were to be improved among the foothills north of Chattanooga to allow Sherman's troops to march rapidly to their crossing sites opposite South Chickamauga Creek. Smith, meanwhile, would assemble every available pontoon to ferry the soldiers across the Tennessee River. Once over, Sherman was to launch the main attack against Bragg's right flank, pushing on along the railroad toward Cleveland to cut the Rebel line of communications. Simultaneously, Thomas would advance directly against Missionary Ridge to pin down the bulk of the Confederate forces. Reliable intelligence suggested Bragg expected that any attack would come against his left flank. To encourage this misconception, when Sherman reached Whiteside's he was to divert his lead division in the direction of Trenton; with the rest of his command he would continue on toward Chattanooga over concealed roads. On the day of the attack —perhaps in deference to Thomas's desires—Hooker was to assault Lookout Mountain and, if possible, carry it and drive on to Rossville, to be poised to cut off a Confederate retreat southward.

Sherman reached Chattanooga on the evening of the fourteenth. The next

morning he, Grant, Thomas, and Smith rode out to the hill opposite South Chickamauga Creek from which Smith earlier had "spied out the land." Leaving Grant and Thomas at the base of the hill, Smith and Sherman climbed to the top. Smith pointed out the portion of Missionary Ridge that Sherman was to seize. Could the Ohioan carry it before Bragg was able to concentrate a force to resist him? Smith wondered. Sherman swept the country with his field glass. Yes, he said, he could take the ridge; what's more, he could seize it by 9:00 A.M. on the appointed day.

The party returned to headquarters. Perhaps swayed by Sherman, who of course wanted every unit he could muster to carry out his mission, Grant withdrew his support for Thomas's plan to take Lookout Mountain.

Sherman's successful crossing of the Tennessee River north of Chattanooga depended on secrecy and exacting preparations. For the latter, Grant and Sherman looked to Baldy Smith. Once again, he was up to the task. The Vermonter laid out for Sherman his concept of the operation. Sherman's command was to go into camp among the foothills north of Chattanooga, hidden from view. One

brigade was to encamp beside the mouth off North Chickamauga Creek. There Smith would assemble his pontoons and float this brigade downriver to secure a landing just below the mouth of South Chickamauga Creek. There engineers would throw across a bridge over which the rest of Sherman's force would cross.

Sherman's immediate objective was to turn Bragg's flank, which meant seizing that portion of Missionary Ridge between Tunnel Hill and South Chickamauga Creek. If successful, Sherman would gain control of the two railroads leading east out of Chattanooga. Loss of the rail lines, over which supplies flowed to the Confederate army, would compel Bragg "either to weaken his lines elsewhere or lose his connection with his base at Chickamauga Station," said Grant. At best, it would force him to withdraw altogether.

Longstreet's departure did little to improve either Bragg's mood or his clarity of thought. Bragg had decided to hold onto his line around Chattanooga, the strength or tactical value of which, now that Federal supplies and troops were flowing into the city unimpeded, was illusory. To do so, Bragg had slightly under 40,000 infantry and only 500 cavalry, which ruled out rapid reconnaissance beyond his flanks.

Having given up Lookout Valley as

lost, Bragg opted to defend the mountain itself. On November 9, General Hardee examined the mountain with Brigadier General John Jackson, temporarily in command of Cheatham's division while the Tennessean was on leave. It had fallen to Jackson to defend Lookout Mountain. Their reconnaissance gave Hardee and Jackson little comfort. "It was agreed on all hands that the position was one extremely difficult to defense against a strong force of the enemy advancing under cover of a heavy fire," said Jackson.

On November 12, Bragg placed Carter Stevenson in command of the overall defense of Lookout and transferred his division to the summit of the mountain. Jackson was to hold the bench with his

THE TENNESSEE RIVER ACTED AS A RIVER HIGHWAY FOR FEDERAL SUPPLIES AND MATERIALS. THIS 1864 PHOTOGRAPH SHOWS SOLDIERS AND CITIZENS WATCHING A STEAMER GO UPRIVER.

(NA)

A POST-BATTLE PHOTOGRAPH OF UNION ARMY TRANSPORTS ON THE TENNESSEE RIVER BELOW CHATTANOOGA.

(LC)

"A VICTORIOUS LITTLE BATTERY"

The northern end of Lookout Mountain loomed over the best transportation routes into Chattanooga. Its bluffs overshadowed the channel of the Tennessee River. At the mountain's base, just above the river, ran the trackage of the Nashville & Chattanooga Railroad. Above the bluffs, on a natural but improved rock shelf, was the main road, the Wauhatchie Pike. Higher still were other less used routes, including the old Federal Road.

Despite the importance of these avenues and Lookout's commanding position over them, Rosecrans was forced to abandon the mountain to the Confederates when he withdrew into Chattanooga following the Battle of Chickamauga. His army could not maintain a line that encompassed both the city and the mountain.

Geography, however, gave the Federals an opportunity to provide added security to their lines around the city and, most important, made it difficult for the Confederates to possess the mountain. Moccasin Point, the great land form created by the hairpin bend of the Tennessee as it flowed westward from Chattanooga, was the key. Moccasin Point offered excellent positions for artillery; the guns the Federals placed on the hills at the southern end of Stringers Ridge were like a dagger thrust forward to keep the Confederates at arm's length. Dug into an extensive series of earthen and log fortifications, the guns of the 10th Indiana Battery and the 18th Ohio Light Artillery commanded much ground from their fortified hilltops. Should the Confederates attempt to attack the Federal lines around Chattanooga from the south, the guns could fire into the flank of the force as it moved to the assault. Should they attempt to cross the Tennessee from near the base of Lookout Mountain to strike Rosecrans's remaining supply link, the guns commanded the best crossings. Most important, the Indianans' and Ohioans' guns on Moccasin Point denied the Confederates easy movement across the tip of Lookout Mountain. The routes of the several roads and almost the entirety of the northern tip of the mountain were within range of the Moccasin Point batteries. They challenged and prevented the movement of men and supplies in any but small numbers over the tip of

own brigade and those of Edward Walthall and John C. Moore.

Commanders elsewhere along Bragg's tenuous front also questioned the defensibility of their positions. Breckinridge, in command of the center and right, was left to defend a position five miles long with just over 16,000 troops. After a bit of shuffling about, Stewart's division finally settled into position in the soggy fields of Chattanooga Valley, from the east bank of Chattanooga Creek to the base of Missionary Ridge. William B. Bate's division and that of Patton Anderson were arrayed behind breastworks of logs and earth along the western base of the ridge. Cleburne's division held the right just south of Tunnel Hill. Pickets from each command were shaken out a mile closer to the Federal entrenchments. A few batteries were left up on the ridge, but no one thought to dig them in.

Patton Anderson was appalled at the sorry state of his sector. "This line of defense, following its sinuosities, was over two miles in length—nearly twice as long as the number of bayonets in the division could adequately defend." Watching the ever-growing number of the mountain in daylight. Even single wagons were potential targets. Sam Divine, a young civilian in Chattanooga during the siege, remembered:

"On one occasion I witnessed a very daring feat made by a teamster driving a four-mule team drawing a wagon . . . . The gunners discovered him as soon as he reached the level of the plateau and fired . . . . I saw every shell when it burst and watched the progress of the race till it was ended . . . . The most critical time was when he reached the open spaces directly in front of the battery, where the road was extremely narrow and there was a precipice of several hundred feet perpendicular down to the railroad track below . . . . When he appeared at the opening he had the throttle wide open and those rebel mules were racing against cannonball time. Boom! Boom! Boom! went six rifled guns; pow! pow! pow! echoed the bursting shells against old Lookout's ribs, but Johnny Reb had beat'em to it and was happy on his way down the other side."

Confederate activities around Robert Cravens's white house on the mountain's slope brought it under fire. Colonel John Bratton of the 6th South

EARTHWORKS ON MOCCASIN BEND.

(NPS)

Carolina writing from there on November 3, 1863, said:

"My Qrs. are in the Craven House . . . . The enemy gave it a shelling the other day while we were passing this point to support Gen. Law who was having a brush with the enemy and again since. There are two or three holes through the room where I am sitting. The Mocasin Battery which you have seen in the papers, does this work."

For the Confederates, this Federal fire meant they could supply and maintain only a single brigade in Lookout Valley west of the mountain, a force too small to hold the area.

When the Federals seized Brown's Ferry and Lookout Valley on October 27 and 28, 1863, they did so without a serious challange from the Southerners. The Moccasin Point batteries prevented practical and timely Confederate reinforcements. A month later, during the Battle of Lookout Mountain, the batteries supported Joseph Hooker's assault by firing into the Confederate positions from the rear and flank as the Federals swept the Southerners around the northern tip of the mountain.

The Moccasin Point batteries had helped hold the Confederates at bay and then throw them back from the Gateway to the Deep South.

Nature favored the Confederates at this juncture, but part of the blame for the delay during the final leg of the march rested on Sherman's shoulders.

Federal campfires, many Confederate troops did more than just ruminate—they gave up the game as lost and walked across the valley under cover of darkness to surrender.

The slow going of Sherman's command gave wavering Rebels ample time to contemplate desertion. The Ohioan had started promptly enough. He lost no time in pushing Ewing's division toward Trenton to make the agreed-upon demonstration against the Confederate left rear in Lookout Valley. To Sherman's chagrin, the march of the main column did not proceed apace. Struggling along through

cold rains and bitter winds over icy wagon roads, his other three divisions made miserable time between Winchester and Bridgeport.

Nature favored the Confederates at this juncture, but part of the blame for the delay during the final leg of the march rested on Sherman's shoulders. Three weeks earlier, Thomas wisely had suggested to Hooker that he leave his wagons while he marched from Bridgeport to Chattanooga; he had had the good sense to act on Thomas's recommendation. But Sherman decided to march with his trains. It was a terrible miscalculation. Wagons

sank in the mire, slowing the march to a crawl.

Grant was beside himself. Burnside had fallen back onto his defenses at Knoxville with Longstreet in close pursuit. Although Burnside was confident he could resist a few days longer, the War Department was frantic for Grant to act. That, of course, he could not do without Sherman. Grant had hoped to begin offensive operations on November 21. By the evening of the twentieth, however, only one brigade of Sherman's command had crossed the pontoon bridge at Brown's Ferry. Grant rescheduled the attack for November 22. Again Sherman was unready. All of John Smith's division had crossed the Tennessee River and gone into camp north of Chattanooga, but Morgan Smith was only partially over, and Ewing had barely reached Hooker's line north of Wauhatchie.

When Grant postponed the attack again—this time until November 23—Thomas renewed his pleas that Hooker be allowed to keep Howard's corps and attack Lookout Mountain. Thomas was worried that Sherman's three days of floundering about in Lookout Valley might have tipped Grant's hand and that Bragg would strengthen his right flank.

Grant rejected Thomas's plan—Sherman would make the main attack against the Rebel right, regardless of when he came up. Bragg had done nothing to strengthen his right; Ewing's display in the upper Lookout Valley had deceived him into thinking that Sherman would attack his left. Even after Sherman's main body and Howard's corps crossed Brown's Ferry, Bragg misjudged the Federal objective. He assumed correctly that Grant was trying to drive a wedge between his army and Longstreet's corps, but he guessed wrong as to where it would be driven. Bragg concluded that Grant was sending Sherman against Longstreet, rather than to strike his own right flank. On this assumption, Bragg weakened his lines even more. On November 22, he ordered Cleburne to withdraw his own and Buckner's divisions from the line and march them to

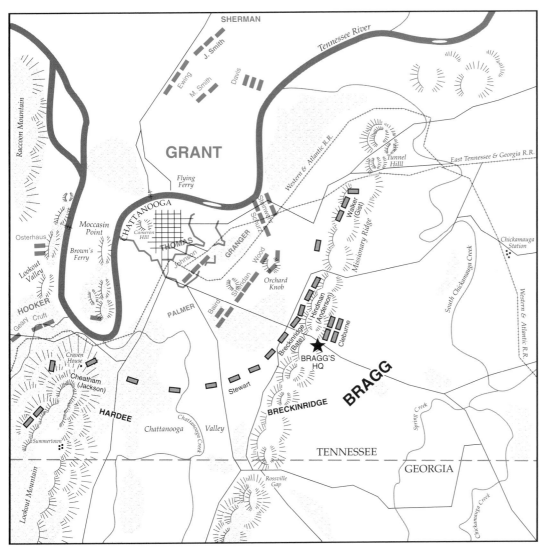

ORCHARD KNOB IN
FEDERAL POSSES-
SION, NOVEMBER 23

On November 23,
Grant ordered
Thomas to conduct
a demonstration
against the
Confederate picket
line. The point select-
ed was Orchard
Knob. At 1:30 P.M.,
Wood's and
Sheridan's divisions
of Granger's 4th
Corps advanced
from the Federal
lines around
Chattanooga and
took Orchard Knob
from the surprised
Confederates.

The Federal attack
caused Bragg to
recall Cleburne's
Division. Cleburne
bivouacked for the
night north of
Bragg's headquarters.
The Confederates
also began to con-
struct fortifications
on the crest of
Missionary Ridge.

Sherman's troops,
encamped out of
sight behind
hills north of
Chattanooga, pre-
pared to move to the
point selected for
their crossing of the
Tennessee River just
downstream from the
mouth of South
Chickamauga Creek.

Chickamauga Station, where they would board cars to join Longstreet.

Bragg had opted to slice away 11,000 more men from his small army at precisely the moment Sherman was reinforcing Grant with nearly twice that number.

Colonel Aquila Wiley of Hazen's brigade saw a surprising sight at sunset on November 22. "Three columns are visible moving up Missionary Ridge on three different roads. I should think the columns consist of at least a brigade of 1,000 men each," Wiley reported to Hazen. General Wood had also been watching the "singular and mysterious" movement across the valley.

Wood and Wiley had witnessed the withdrawal of Cleburne's division. They reported the sighting through the chain of command to Grant's headquarters, along with the claims of two deserters that the Confederate army was falling back.

Grant took Wood's message seriously. Deserters on Phil Sheridan's front had said the same thing. If the Rebel army was withdrawing, Grant reasoned, it was imperative that he disrupt Bragg's movement to prevent him from reinforcing Longstreet. Before dawn, he instructed Thomas to drive the enemy pickets from his front in order to force the Confederates to reveal the strength of their main line. Since the best evidence of the enemy's departure had come from Wood's sector, Thomas charged him with conducting the reconnaissance. The orders were unambiguous: Wood was to avoid a collision with the enemy and return to his fortifications after completing the reconnaissance.

Daylight on November 23 revealed the immediate objective of Wood's foray: a craggy knoll, two thousand yards east of

A VIEW OF MISSIONARY
RIDGE FROM
ORCHARD KNOB
SHORTLY AFTER
THE BATTLE.

(LC)

Fort Wood, known as Orchard Knob. Rising sharply one hundred feet above the Chattanooga Valley, the knob was covered with small trees and a line of rifle pickets occupied by Rebel picket reserves.

Under chilly but crystal blue autumn skies, Wood's 8,000 infantrymen marched out of their entrenchments and formed ranks with parade ground precision. Phil Sheridan's division, under orders to protect Wood's right flank, lined up with equal exactitude. On Wood's left, Howard's Eleventh Corps extended the Federal line to Citico Creek.

By 1:15 P.M., nearly 20,000 bluecoats stood at attention in the broad valley between the opposing picket lines. Grant, Thomas, Hooker, Howard, and Assistant Secretary of War Charles Dana all came out to watch the performance.

At 1:30 P.M., buglers blew the command "Forward," and Wood's and Sheridan's long lines sprang forward at the double-quick time. The Federal infantry swept across the plain, covering 800 yards before the stunned Rebels opened fire. Before they could reload, Yankee skirmishers were upon them, rounding up prisoners and pursuing the rest toward the knob.

Six hundred bewildered Rebels confronted the advance of nearly 14,000 Federals. They exacted a heavy toll on the attackers, but the issue was never in doubt. Those Southerners not shot or captured retreated to the base of Missionary Ridge.

A few minutes before 3:00 P.M., Wood signaled General Thomas: "I have carried the first line of the enemy's entrenchments." What were Thomas's instructions?

Grant and Thomas consulted briefly. Both hesitated: Wood had done far more than conduct a mere reconnaissance; should he be recalled as planned? Rawlins broke the impasse: "It will have a bad effect to let them come back and try it over again." Grant took the advice: "Intrench them and send up support," he told Thomas.

As the sun set and a deep chill fell over the valley, Bragg emerged from his daze. He readjusted his lines and recalled every unit within a day's march to meet what he now realized was a serious threat against his unprotected right. Cleburne's division, which had not yet boarded the cars at Chickamauga Station, returned after dark. General Joseph Lewis's Kentucky "Orphan Brigade" came in from guard duty at Chickamauga Station. Marcus Wright's Tennessee Brigade returned from Charleston by rail.

To shore up his right, Bragg stripped his left over the protest of Carter Stevenson, who still believed the real threat was against Lookout Mountain. Bragg wisely ignored Stevenson and ordered William H. T. Walker's division to withdraw from the base of Lookout Mountain and move along Missionary Ridge to the far right, taking position a quarter mile south of Tunnel Hill. To command this now critical sector, Bragg called upon William Hardee, who turned over the extreme left to Stevenson.

Stevenson assumed command of affairs west of Chattanooga Creek reluctantly. He sent a brigade of Jackson's division and Cummings's brigade to close the gap in the valley that Walker's departure had opened. He told Walthall to deploy his 1,500 Mississippians so as to picket the mountain and retain a reserve sufficient to help Moore hold the main line near the Cravens house.

Having done what he felt he could for the left and right, Bragg turned his attention to the center of the army, which he had entrusted to Breckinridge. After two months in front of Chattanooga, the two generals finally realized that it might be prudent to fortify the crest of Missionary Ridge. Breckinridge ordered Bate to begin digging at daylight. Hardee told Anderson to do likewise. Both Hardee and Breckinridge recalled their cannon from the valley, while their chiefs of artillery tried in the dark to select the firing positions they should have reconnoitered weeks earlier.

Neither Bragg, Breckinridge, nor Hardee apparently was ready to commit himself entirely to the defense of the crest of Missionary Ridge should an attack come against the center. Unable to decide between holding the existing rifle pits at the foot of the ridge or withdrawing to the unfortified crest, they settled on a

peculiar compromise: Bate and Anderson were ordered to recall half their divisions on the crest and to leave the remainder in the rifle pits along the base. Stewart, meanwhile, was told to stretch his already attenuated line a bit farther to the right, so as to rest at the foot of Missionary Ridge a half mile south of Bragg's headquarters.

Bragg may have gone to bed that night satisfied with his dispositions. In part, his instincts had been correct. The right needed reinforcing, and quickly. But in his zeal to do so, he had left Stevenson with too few troops to hold the left. And although he at last had begun to strengthen the crest of Missionary Ridge, Bragg's and Breckinridge's decision to split the Kentuckian's corps between the top and the base negated any advantage the high ground might offer.

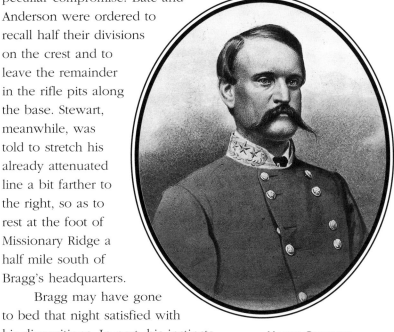

MAJOR GENERAL
JOHN C. BRECKINRIDGE

(LC)

Thomas was as pleased as Grant with the events of November 23. Not only had his army proven to Grant that it could fight, but he had won a concession from the commanding general. Hard use and rising waters had torn apart the pontoon bridge at Brown's Ferry, stranding the last of Sherman's units, Brigadier General Peter Osterhaus's division, in Lookout Valley. When it became clear that Osterhaus would be unable to cross for at least twelve hours, Grant ordered him to report to Hooker. The brigades of Walter Whitaker and William Grose were also trapped in Lookout Valley.

The three divisions now congregating in Lookout Valley were more than

LIEUTENANT GENERAL WILLIAM J. HARDEE

(BL)

enough for a simple diversion against the Confederates, so Grant acceded to Thomas's demand that a more serious effort be made against Lookout Mountain. He stopped short of giving permission for a full-scale assault; Hooker, he cautioned, should "take the point only if his demonstration should develop its practicability."

Such subtleties were lost on Hooker. In his orders to Geary for November 24, Hooker said nothing of a mere demonstration; Geary was to take Lookout Mountain, plain and simple. He was to set off at dawn, cross Lookout Creek above Wauhatchie, and march down the valley, "sweeping every Rebel from it." Whitaker's brigade would accompany

camps to their assigned staging areas. The brigade of Brigadier General Giles Smith was to take to the boats in North Chickamauga Creek. Joseph Lightburn's brigade of the same division and Ewing's division were to assemble behind the high hills opposite South Chickamauga Creek.

The operation was to begin at midnight. Giles Smith's brigade was to float down the Tennessee, land just above South Chickamauga Creek, and then disarm the Rebel pickets posted near its mouth. After Smith's men disembarked, the empty boats would bring over the rest of Sherman's force. Lightburn's brigade and John Smith's division were to

SHERMAN WAS TO CROSS THE TENNESSEE RIVER NEAR THIS POINT.

(USAMHI)

him; Grose's brigade and Osterhaus's division would cross the creek near its mouth. The two forces were to converge on the point of Lookout. Once he controlled the mountain, Hooker intended to drive his united command through Chattanooga Valley against Bragg's extreme left near Rossville.

Sherman declined Grant's offer to delay the offensive one day more to allow Osterhaus to rejoin his corps; Sherman was sure he could succeed with the three divisions on hand.

During the afternoon, Sherman's troops marched from their concealed

entrench on high ground along the east bank of the river, while Ewing's division was ferried over.

Once everybody was organized on the east bank, the three divisions would advance against the northern extreme of Missionary Ridge.

The crossing began on schedule, and by 6:30 A.M. Sherman had two divisions assembled less than two miles from Missionary Ridge. A mile and a half to the south, General Howard was preparing to send Bushbeck's brigade north along the river road to open communications with him. And John Smith had discovered a

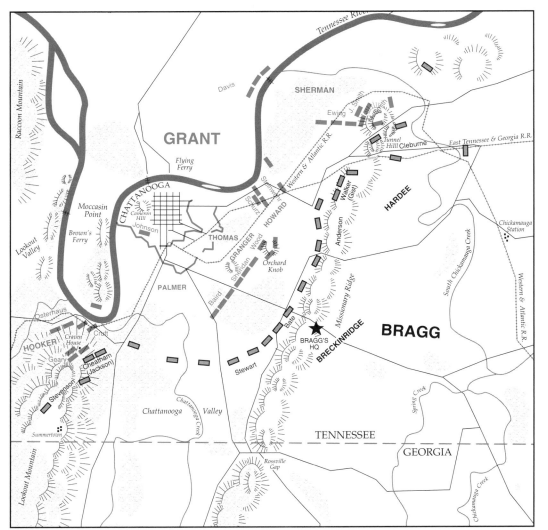

Federal troops under Sherman began crossing the Tennessee River just below the mouth of South Chickamauga Creek before dawn. That afternoon, Sherman advanced toward the north end of Missionary Ridge to attack the Confederate right flank but found the topography and Confederate troop dispositions different than what had been expected. Sherman was not successful in rolling up the Confederate right.

On the Confederate left, Federals under Hooker attacked and drove the Confederates from the slopes of Lookout Mountain. Geary's and Cruft's divisions swept northward toward and around the northern tip of the mountain. Joined by Osterhaus's Division, they drove the Confederates before them and forced the Southerners to abandon their remaining positions on Lookout Mountain that night.

second, more commanding ridge 500 yards east of the one he had fortified. He seized it without opposition. Not a single Rebel could be seen in the fields to his front. At a minimum, a strong reconnaissance into the woods beyond seemed in order. Yet Sherman hesitated, unwilling to move until Ewing was up. He told Smith to fortify the ridge, and the morning slipped quietly away.

Bragg was in the saddle shortly after daybreak. He rode north along Missionary Ridge examining his lines with satisfaction when, through the lifting fog, he saw, two miles across the valley, the divisions of John Smith and Morgan Smith digging in at the mouth of South Chickamauga Creek and Bushbeck's brigade filing north to join them.

No doubt Bragg was stunned. He had not expected a movement against his right emanating from a point so far to the north. But even now, with proof of Grant's intentions there before him, Bragg faltered; perhaps Sherman's crossing was merely a feint. The measures he took during the morning were stopgaps, reflecting an uncertainty as profound as that of Sherman. Bragg had ample troops at hand with which to contest Sherman's advance: Cleburne's division, reinforced by the Orphan Brigade, lay bivouacked behind Bragg's headquarters. But Bragg told Cleburne to send only one brigade to the far right. When Marcus Wright's brigade reached Chickamauga Station at 8:30 A.M., Bragg ordered him to march to the mouth of South Chickamauga Creek to "resist any enemy attempt to cross"—a bizarre order since Sherman already had five times as many troops over as Wright had in his brigade.

Bragg did nothing more. Only two brigades, neither within supporting distance of the other, moved to resist an advance by three divisions, supported by a fourth under Brigadier General Jefferson C. Davis.

Bragg had handed Sherman the chance to destroy his army; the Ohioan let it slip through his fingers. As the morning passed, he kept the two Smiths busy digging in while waiting for Ewing to cross the river. Howard cantered up to the head of Bushbeck's column at noon. Less certain that he could succeed without reinforcements, Sherman convinced Howard to leave Bushbeck with him.

At 1:30 P.M., with less than four hours of gray daylight remaining, Sherman advanced. Less than a mile and a half of fields, forest, and swamps stood between Sherman and the high hills at the northern extreme of Missionary Ridge. Displaying uncommon trepidation, Sherman moved at a snail's pace, constantly looking to his right for any sign of Rebels bounding down from Missionary Ridge to take him in the flank.

But there was not a Confederate within two miles of Sherman's flank. Before noon, Bragg had ridden off toward Lookout Mountain without taking any further action to strengthen his right. Nor did Hardee act until Sherman's massed Federals marched out into the fields, at which time he ordered Cleburne to move his remaining three brigades with all haste toward the right of Missionary Ridge, "near the point where the [railroad] tunnel passes through."

GENERAL
WILLIAM T. SHERMAN

(NPS)

The nexus of the line Hardee hoped to hold with Gist and Cleburne was Tunnel Hill (so named by Cleburne in his report). The highest point along the northern stretch of Missionary Ridge, Tunnel Hill rose 250 yards north of the Chattanooga and Cleveland Railroad tunnel. The next piece of ground to the north were two detached hills that formed a U-shaped eminence much higher than Tunnel Hill.

Cleburne had just inspected the ground around Tunnel Hill when a courier announced that the Yankees were marching up the far slope of the eastern hill. Cleburne ordered the Texas Brigade of Brigadier General James Smith across Tunnel Hill and up the near slope of the detached hill. In a ravine between the elevations, the Texans collided with Yankee skirmishers. Smith halted on the summit of Tunnel Hill and kept the Federals occupied while Cleburne deployed the rest of his division. He arrayed Mark Lowrey's brigade to the left of Smith and sent Daniel Govan to the east-west spur north of the railroad to protect Smith's right flank and rear.

Sherman's actions in the first crucial minutes after contact was made were deplorable. He had made a terrible error. Through a combination of poor maps and negligent reconnaissance, Sherman had marched from the river convinced that the detached hills were the northern extreme of Missionary Ridge. Not until the lead brigades of his three divisions consolidated on the summit of the eastern hill did Sherman, looking toward Smith's Texans drawn up on Tunnel Hill, realize his mistake. With fifty minutes of daylight remaining—enough time to have driven Cleburne's badly attenuated line across the railroad and probably have forced Bragg to abandon his entire Missionary Ridge position—Sherman chose the safe course: he ordered his men to dig in for the night.

Fighting Joe Hooker had not the

slightest doubt that he could take Lookout Mountain. Scouts, deserters, and simple observation had given him an excellent feel for Confederate dispositions, numerical strength, and vulnerabilities. Hooker dismissed any direct attempt at dislodging Stevenson from the summit; his position there would become untenable, in any case, once Hooker swept around the bench.

Hooker and his staff worked until after midnight perfecting their plans. Attention to detail was imperative, as Hooker's force consisted of three divisions from three different corps, none of which had fought together before.

At 3:00 A.M. on November 24, Geary received his orders to "cross Lookout Creek and to assault Lookout Mountain, marching down the valley and sweeping every rebel from it." He was to break camp at daylight. Colonel Whitaker got his orders at the same time. He roused his men at 4:00 A.M. for the two-hour march to Wauhatchie, where they would join up with Geary. Colonel Grose was instructed to effect a lodgment on the far bank

of Lookout Creek near the mouth. To General Osterhaus went a supporting role. Williamson's brigade was to protect the artillery that Hooker was gathering on the hills near the mouth of Lookout Creek; Woods's brigade would cover Grose and cross the creek after him, then ascend the slope and form a junction with the left of Geary's division as it worked its way around the mountain.

Hooker left little to chance. During the night, he brought forward all available artillery to pulverize the Rebel pickets and cover the advance of his own infantry. By daybreak, he had nine batteries lined up

between Light's Mill and the mouth of Lookout Creek. Two batteries from the Army of the Cumberland lent their support from Moccasin Point; two others set up near Chattanooga Creek.

General Walthall had no idea that a quarter of Grant's artillery was trained on his brigade, but he could feel the cold tingle of impending calamity in the misty dawn air. General Moore was even more pessimistic than Walthall: "No serious effort has been made to construct defensive works for our forces on the mountain."

The man in overall command, Carter Stevenson, could offer his subordinates little. He was unfamiliar with the ground and was not even sure that Bragg really wanted him to stay on the mountain.

Dawn came at 6:30 A.M. High water and a fast current delayed Geary's crossing of Lookout Creek until 8:30 A.M. The fog had thickened, observed Geary with satisfaction: "Drifting clouds enveloped the whole ridge of the mountain top, and heavy mists and fogs obscured the slope from lengthened vision."

Colonel George Cobham's brigade filed across a footbridge over Lookout Creek first. Next over was Colonel David Ireland, whose brigade faced to the front midway up the slope to form the center of Geary's line of battle. Colonel Charles Candy's brigade crossed the creek next and extended Geary's left down to the base of the mountain. Walter Whitaker brought his brigade over Lookout Creek last and formed 300 yards to the rear of Geary.

A little after 9:30 A.M., the bugles sounded "Forward" and Geary's skirmishers disappeared into the fog and timber. For nearly an hour the Federals slipped and stumbled along the craggy western slope of Lookout. Finally, at 10:30 A.M., the rattle of musketry from the skirmish line announced that contact had been made. Geary's skirmishers had struck Walthall's pickets one mile southwest of the point. The Rebels held on, but their line was stretched far too thin to offer prolonged resistance. Geary's main line came up without much trouble, and the pressure on the Mississippians became unbearable. As the Federals closed to within a few yards, the Rebels broke. Dozens were hit, and scores more surrendered.

A little after 9:30 A.M., the bugles sounded "Forward" and Geary's skirmishers disappeared into the fog and timber. For nearly an hour the Federals slipped and stumbled along the craggy western slope of Lookout.

THE BATTLE OF LOOKOUT MOUNTAIN, THE SCENE FROM LOOKOUT VALLEY ILLUSTRATION BY THEODORE R. DAVIS.

(LC)

As Geary's line came in sight and the Rebel pickets began trickling from their breastworks, Hooker ordered his artillery to saturate the enemy's line of retreat along the mountainside. Hooker's intentions were good but, up in the dusky forest toward which his cannoneers trained their pieces, the opposing lines were on top of one another. Smoke and fog hid the action from those in the valley, making the aim of the artillerymen uncertain at best.

About 11:30 A.M., the wild Yankee pursuit came to an abrupt halt 300 yards southwest of the point of Lookout Mountain when Ireland and Cobham ran into Walthall's two-regiment reserve, posted between the base of the cliff and the Cravens house. Though badly outnumbered, the Mississippians gave a good account of themselves, throwing back Ireland's first attempt at storming their works.

With Geary and his staff on foot far to the rear, Ireland and Cobham acted on their own to meet this unexpected resistance. Outnumbered four to one and outflanked on both the right and left, Walthall's second line of resistance disintegrated. Walthall tried to rally the men, but few paid him any attention. All order was lost as the Mississippians spilled rearward, past Walthall, around the point of the mountain, and back toward the Cravens house.

At 12:10 P.M. Ireland and Cobham rounded the point of Lookout Mountain and drove eastward along the bench toward the Cravens house.

The Federals kept on past the Cravens house after Walthall's survivors, who were disappearing into the fog. Uncertain of what lurked in the mist-shrouded trees beyond the Cravens place, Ireland's New Yorkers wheeled to the right and trod southeastward along the slope. Off to their left were Chattanooga Valley and the entrenchments of the Army of the Cumberland.

Geary's appearance below the point of Lookout Mountain at noon was the signal for Hooker to set in motion the brigades of Charles Woods and William Grose, which were poised on the west bank of Lookout Creek, ready to cross a footbridge. While Cobham and Ireland cleared the upper reaches of the mountain, Candy's brigade swept the ground between the base of Lookout Mountain and the east bank of the creek.

Shortly before noon, Candy passed through the marshy field opposite the footbridge, clearing the way for Woods and Grose. Woods advanced eastward, while Grose ascended the slope. The belated advance of Woods and Grose

yards south of the Cravens house. Ninety minutes had passed before Moore received an answer from Mudwall Jackson to a 9:30 A.M. inquiry asking where he should deploy his brigade. Jackson was incredulous: Did Moore not recall the plan of the night before to defend the line at the Cravens house? Moore was reluctant to move. He applied to Walthall for reassurances that the Mississippian would be on his left when Moore brought his own brigade forward. Walthall could not answer—he was being overwhelmed too quickly to promise anything.

spelled doom for the last of Walthall's regiments. Crouched behind the railroad embankment near the turnpike bridge, the Thirty-fourth Mississippi was cut off from the forces on the bench by the Federal crossing, and virtually the entire regiment surrendered. With them were 200 men from Moore's picket line, taken from behind by Woods.

General Moore caught a glimpse of his picket line withering, but he had more pressing concerns on the bench, where the remainder of his brigade stood, 400

There was bungling aplenty among the Confederate commanders on Lookout Mountain, but no one displayed greater negligence than Jackson. He remained glued to his headquarters, a mile behind the line he had been charged to defend. Jackson lacked even the presence of mind to call for reinforcements; Stevenson had to offer them. When the roll of rifle volleys announced Walthall's clash with Geary at 12:30 P.M., Stevenson ordered Brigadier General Edmund Pettus to take

three of his regiments down from the summit and report to Jackson.

By then, Moore was moving. As they neared the Cravens yard, his Alabamians met the remnants of Walthall's brigade rushing to the rear. Instead of finding the stone wall to their front, Moore and his men glimpsed Ireland's New Yorkers through the drizzle. Both sides opened fire at a range of 100 yards. The thick mist disguised Moore's small numbers, and the New Yorkers retreated beyond the stone wall. Moore settled his men in behind it and in the rifle pits it screened.

Moore put up a good fight. He stretched his 1,000 men as thin as he felt he could behind the entrenchments, from the Cravens house down the mountainside, and awaited the Yankee counterattack.

It was slow in coming. Ireland's men were dazed and tired. They lay down along the western fringe of the Cravens yard, protected from Moore's fire by the fog and a dip in the ground.

Whitaker's brigade arrived behind Ireland's stalled line a little after 1:00 P.M. His men were spoiling for a fight, and they swept over the supine New Yorkers and into the yard.

Moore was woefully outnumbered —Whitaker alone had 500 more men than he did—and the odds were getting worse. To Moore's right front, Candy's brigade was clambering up the mountainside to regain its connection with Ireland's left. To Candy's left and rear were the brigades of Woods and Grose. Although not yet near enough to attack Moore, the Federal line clearly extended far beyond his right flank: "It became evident we must either fall back or be surrounded and captured," surmised Moore. He chose the former course and withdrew most of his command off in good order southward, toward the Summertown road.

Their front clear, Whitaker's men whooped and hopped over the stone wall. Whitaker wanted to stop there, but his men surged past him. Ireland was on the move again as well, to the left and rear of Whitaker.

Whitaker was not alone in wanting to call a halt. As the weather worsened, Hooker was content merely to see Geary round the bench. Fearful that the enemy might be reinforced and his own lines disordered by the fog and rugged ground, he had sent word to Geary to halt for the day before reaching the Cravens house. But Geary was on foot and too far behind his troops to stop them, and so, as Hooker put it, "fired by success, with a flying, panic-stricken enemy before them, they pressed impetuously forward."

The fog slowed them, giving Moore the chance to get away and Walthall time to form a scratch line 300 yards south of the Cravens house with the 600 men left to him. Crouching behind boulders and fallen trees, they kept up enough of a racket to halt Whitaker. Thirty minutes later, they heard the tramp of Pettus's column coming up behind them.

Pettus filed his three Alabama regiments off the Cravens house road and into line. Marching forward, they relieved Walthall's band a little after 2:00 P.M. and fell in behind a natural breastwork of limestone outcrop. Moore regrouped on their right.

Pettus's line was engaged instantly. For the rest of the afternoon and well into the night, the six Alabama regiments of

THIS ILLUSTRATION FROM *HARPER'S WEEKLY* WAS TITLED *GENERAL HOOKER FIGHTING AMONG THE CLOUDS.*

(LC)

Pettus and Moore traded volleys with an invisible foe. In some places, the two lines were just thirty yards apart. At points of collision, the smoke of battle hung in blue sheets among the naked branches of the trees until beaten into nothing by the falling rain. The fighting degenerated into a series of weak, half-blind punches and counterpunches in the foggy twilight. The racket was tremendous, the lead expended prodigious, but hardly anyone was hurt.

Fighting Joe Hooker's confidence returned an hour before sunset. Although he had told Geary earlier to dig in for the night along the eastern slope, Hooker now announced to Grant his intention to descend into Chattanooga Valley as soon as the fog lifted. "In all probability the enemy will evacuate tonight. His line of retreat is seriously threatened by my troops."

A MODERN-DAY VIEW FROM ATOP LOOKOUT MOUNTAIN.

(NPS)

The fog never lifted, so Hooker was not put to the test. Hooker may have embarrassed himself with his blustering, but he had correctly guessed Bragg's intentions.

Down in Chattanooga Valley, Bragg was furious—at a loss to understand how Stevenson, with six brigades at his disposal, could have failed to hold the bench and slope of Lookout Mountain. Now Stevenson was begging for another

brigade in order to avert total defeat. Bragg granted the request conditionally—the brigade sent over was to be used to cover Stevenson's withdrawal. Bragg would do no more. To him, the battle effectively was over and Lookout Mountain lost. At 2:30 P.M., he instructed Stevenson to withdraw from the mountain to the east side of Chattanooga Creek.

As Bragg left the timing and manner of the withdrawal to his discretion, Stevenson decided not to risk breaking contact with the Federals on the eastern slope until the troops on the summit made good their escape. Walthall, Pettus, and Moore would have to hold on—all night if necessary—to keep open the Summertown road, the only means of egress into Chattanooga Valley.

The senseless firing on the mountainside continued, alternately sputtering and swelling. Union regiments were moved in and out of the line during the night so that everyone on the mountain eventually had a hand in the fight.

Down in the valley, near Chattanooga Creek, Breckinridge, Stevenson, Jackson, and the recently returned Ben Franklin Cheatham met at the Gillespie house at 8:00 P.M. Cheatham was livid—Jackson had nearly destroyed two of his brigades. Breckinridge yielded the floor and left, and Cheatham took charge of the meeting. He concluded the business rapidly. Cheatham told Stevenson to remove his own and Cheatham's divisions from the west side of Chattanooga Creek and stand by on the east bank while Cheatham searched out Bragg for further orders.

Bragg, meanwhile, was absorbed in a meeting of his own. Breckinridge had ridden directly from the Gillespie house to army headquarters. There he, Bragg, and Hardee fell into a largely futile discussion of how they might recoup their losses of the day. The situation was grim. With Lookout Mountain lost and Sherman menacing Tunnel Hill, both flanks were in

danger. Another setback on either flank threatened the whole army. Outnumbered two to one, Bragg barely had enough troops to reinforce one flank. Finally, South Chickamauga Creek was swelling rapidly from the steady rains, jeopardizing Bragg's line of retreat.

Bragg had no idea what to do. He turned to Hardee and Breckinridge for advice. Hardee was all for conceding Chattanooga. The army, he said, should cut its losses and withdraw across South Chickamauga Creek. Breckinridge disagreed vehemently. There was no time that night for such a move, which certainly would be discovered. In falling back, Breckinridge continued, the army would be subject to defeat in detail after daybreak. Furthermore, he said, Missionary Ridge was an inherently strong position.

Bragg endorsed Breckinridge's petition to hold fast on Missionary Ridge. Hardee argued a bit longer for a withdrawal but finally

relented. He convinced himself that the natural strength of Missionary Ridge was sufficient to deter a direct assault against the center or left. Hardee decided that the real threat would come from Sherman against the right flank, which he argued was also the most vulnerable part of the Confederate line.

Bragg agreed. He promised to send Cheatham and Stevenson to reinforce the right during the night. Hardee would command the four divisions on the right —those of Cleburne, Walker, Stevenson, and Cheatham. Anderson's division was too far to the left for Hardee to devote

WALKER, THE SOLDIER ARTIST

The striking terrain of the Chattanooga region added a scenic dimension to the fighting for the Gateway to the Deep South. Lofty mountains and ridges loomed over the armies, and the heights offered spectacular views. The November 1863 battles for Chattanooga seemingly took place in a vast, outdoor arena.

The picturesque potential of the battles on Lookout Mountain and Missionary Ridge was not lost on one of the mid-nineteenth century's foremost members of the artistic community—Englishman James Walker. Born in 1818, Walker came to America with his family in 1824. At age nineteen, he moved to Mexico and for a time taught art at the Military College of Tampico. He was living in Mexico City when the Mexican War began and accompanied the American army as an interpreter in the Mexico City campaign. His experiences in Mexico led him to produce a series of paintings chronicling that conflict and brought him national recognition in the United States as a military artist. Acknowledging his talents, Walker received a commission to paint a nine-by-nineteen-foot image of *The Battle of Chapultepec* for the United States Capitol. By the time that work was completed in 1862, the American states were at war with themselves and Walker had another con-

flict to record on canvas. Thereafter, he produced thirty works on the War Between the States encompassing images of camp life, individuals, and several battles, including Gettysburg. It was his work with the Battle of Lookout Mountain or "the Battle Above the Clouds," that gave him lasting recognition.

Walker spent time with the Army of the Cumberland in Chattanooga in early 1864 and was moved to produce a series of works depicting the military action in the area. With an eye for detail and accuracy, Walker carefully studied the battle-fields. He walked and rode over the scene of the engagements, made sketches, and interviewed important Union participants, such as George H. Thomas, Joseph Hooker, Dan Butterfield, and John White Geary. He even employed a photographer to produce images for later reference. "I am confident that I can give our people here in the North a better idea of what has been accomplished down there than any report that can be written. No one can describe Lookout in word painting so as to make it satisfactorily understood," wrote the artist at the conclusion of his Chattanooga visit. From these sources, Walker first produced *The Battle of Chickamauga* and *The Battle of Lookout Mountain* (see back cover), both commissioned

by the United States government. Later, he also produced *Mounted Union Officers on Lookout Mountain, Union Cavalry on Lookout Mountain*, and another version depicting the battle itself.

Walker's second image of the Battle of Lookout Mountain was his largest work and is considered by many to be his masterpiece. Commissioned by "Fighting Joe" Hooker to commemorate that general's part in "The Battle Above the Clouds," this second *Battle of Lookout Mountain* (see below) covers a thirteen-by-thirty-foot canvas and was produced for $20,000 over a four-year period. Upon completion in 1874, the painting toured the country with stops in New York, Philadelphia, and San Francisco. Hooker said of Walker's grandest work, "I wanted it to be the representation of an American battle as it was. . . . You appear to have adhered to the instructions with singular fidelity and success. It is unnecessary for me to speak of the landscape, except in terms of the highest approval. . . . I am equally gratified with the representation of the dramatis personae on your canvas." While later generations of art and military historians would acknowledge greater artistic license than did Hooker, *The Battle of Lookout Mountain* is one of the most visually significant documents on that important engagement.

Following the completion of *The Battle of Lookout Mountain*, Walker turned his artistic attention to a new American arena, the West. Moving to California in 1876, Walker produced more than thirty images of Western life and California scenes before dying in 1889 at age 70.

JAMES WALKER'S SECOND VERSION OF *THE BATTLE OF LOOKOUT MOUNTAIN.*

(NPS)

adequate attention both to it and to the expected fight around Tunnel Hill. Consequently, it was reassigned to Breckinridge. The Kentuckian was to order Stewart up from Chattanooga Valley and onto the ridge at once; responsibility for guarding the extreme left at Rossville Gap would rest with Stewart.

Back at the Gillespie house, Stevenson and Jackson waited patiently for Cheatham to return. It was well after midnight when a courier from Bragg galloped up and announced that all troops west of Chattanooga Creek were to start at once for the far right of the army. No one could find Cheatham so Stevenson took responsibility for the move. Up on the frigid slope of Lookout Mountain, the firing died out a little after midnight.

Hooker's success on Lookout Mountain was of little interest to Grant. In his view, Sherman's march against Bragg's right was the real battle, and on it he pinned his hopes. As darkness fell on November 24, Grant believed his faith in his friend vindicated. Sherman assumed he had carried Tunnel Hill, and Grant based his planning on the impression that Sherman need only press his advantage at daybreak to roll up Bragg's flank and complete his victory.

Grant's instructions to Sherman were simple: he was "to attack the enemy at the point most advantageous from your position at early dawn." To Thomas went a supporting role: "I have instructed Sherman to advance as soon as it is light in the morning, and your attack, which will be simultaneous, will be in co-operation. Your command will either carry the rifle-pits and ridge directly in front of them or move to the left, as the presence of the enemy may require."

Grant envisioned no serious role for Hooker; at best his was to divert Bragg's attention from

his right flank by a further display on Lookout Mountain.

But Thomas flouted Grant's directive. He called Hooker down to the valley, where he could make a more tangible contribution by demonstrating directly against Bragg's left flank on Missionary Ridge. Also, Thomas wanted to ensure that his own right was protected.

By 10:00 A.M., when Hooker got started, Thomas was feeling much relieved. A stunning revelation had compelled Grant both to endorse Thomas's orders to Hooker and to postpone Thomas's own advance toward Missionary Ridge. When the morning fog burned off, Grant and his staff realized that Sherman

36

did not hold Tunnel Hill, which bristled with Confederate cannon and toward which long lines of Rebel infantry were marching. Grant, Thomas, and their staffs waited on Orchard Knob with ill-concealed impatience for Sherman to go into action.

But Sherman was in the throes of indecision. Dawn found him no more capable of grasping the reality of the Confederate presence on Tunnel Hill—or of overcoming it—than he had been at sunset the day before. Neither did he appreciate the overwhelming superiority he enjoyed: facing Sherman's four divisions (16,000 men) was Cleburne's three small brigades, numbering 4,000. And only Smith's Texas brigade actually stood atop Tunnel Hill.

Yet Sherman hesitated. Not until 8:00 A.M., ninety minutes after Sherman should have launched his attack, did his weary men finally receive orders to quit fortifying their fronts. He finally decided to strike Tunnel Hill simultaneously from the north and northwest with just two brigades: those of John Corse and John Loomis of Ewing's division. Corse would come at Tunnel Hill from the northwest. Loomis, on his right, was to approach Tunnel Hill through the open fields between the railroads. To John Smith and Morgan Smith went ill-defined supporting roles; to Jefferson C. Davis went no role at all.

The results of Sherman's poorly planned assault were predictable. Corse ran up against Tunnel Hill with only 920 men and was decimated in two successive charges. Before making a third, Corse wanted to know if Sherman wanted him to try again. "Go back and make that charge immediately; time is everything," Sherman snarled.

Sherman's dawdling was Cleburne's salvation. Every minute the Ohioan delayed brought the Irish immigrant vital reinforcements. The first came just after sunrise, when Brigadier General John Brown's Tennesseans staggered into position. With infantry on hand to support them, the batteries of Calvert and Goldthwaite were wheeled into place above the tunnel. Cumming's brigade showed up next and was fed into line to the left of Brown. Lewis's Orphan Brigade reported to Cleburne next. Cleburne left him behind Smith, on the eastern slope of Tunnel Hill, as a reserve.

At 10:30 A.M., Sherman's cannon unleashed a barrage on Smith's Texans. Behind the exploding shells came Corse's infantry. Lieutenant H. Shannon, in command of Swett's battery atop Tunnel Hill, wheeled his guns to face the bluecoats. He shredded their ranks with canister, but the Yankees kept coming. They charged to within fifty feet of Smith's line before breaking. Smith was dangerously wounded, and brigade command passed to Colonel Hiram Granbury.

Corse had attacked with only a part of his brigade. Before trying again, he called up the remainder and sent to Sherman for help.

But Corse had no intention of waiting for reinforcements before attacking a second time. Placing himself in the front line, at 11:30 A.M. Corse ordered an advance. This time the Yankees came within a few feet of the enemy works before giving way. Corse fell, slightly wounded. While he was carried to the rear, his troops kept up the pressure on the Texans, holding onto the northern slope of Tunnel Hill with a rabid tenacity.

Cleburne worked feverishly to dislodge the Federals. He positioned Douglas's battery near Granbury's right flank to enfilade the Yankee left, then called forward two of Lewis's regiments to extend his line eastward.

When the Federals at last gave way, the Texans surged over their breastworks and into the ravine after them. Regrouping on the rise north of Tunnel Hill, the Yankees beat back the counterattack. Colonel Charles Walcutt, assuming command from Corse, appealed to Sherman for orders.

Sherman had had enough. Corse's setback convinced him that the northern approach to Tunnel Hill was bankrupt so he refused to send Walcutt reinforcements, telling him simply to hold his ground. For all practical purposes, the first Federal effort to take Tunnel Hill was over at noon.

How was it that Cleburne had been free to turn his undivided attention to pulverizing Corse's brigade? Largely because Loomis had taken literally General Ewing's admonition that he "under no circumstances" bring on a general engagement, marching his brigade only as far

as the edge of the woods. Nearly half a mile of meadows and soggy fields lay between Loomis and the railroad tunnel, on top of which Cleburne's artillery stood, ground Loomis was averse to cross.

At 10:30 A.M., Loomis was handed unexpected orders. Corse was about to assault Tunnel Hill, and Loomis was to advance at once in cooperation. Loomis made a good faith effort at complying, but he had no idea where Corse's flank lay or when or in what direction Corse might attack. So Loomis moved out blindly. Guiding on the mouth of the tunnel, he opened a gap of 400 yards between his left and Corse's right.

Loomis never had a chance. The instant his men stepped into the clear, they were easy marks for the two batteries atop the tunnel. The Yankees made it as far as the railroad embankment at a point where it curved south.

Loomis was in trouble. His three regiments behind the embankment were

MAJOR GENERAL PATRICK R. CLEBURNE

(USAMHI)

ALFRED R. WAUD'S postwar drawing of Cleburne's repulse of Sherman at Missionary Ridge.

(NPS)

leaking wounded rearward at an alarming rate, and his left-flank regiment, the Ninetieth Illinois, had the impossible duty of trying to make the connection with Corse. The brigade had strayed too far south, and the Ninetieth had lost so many men that it covered a front barely the width of two normal-sized companies. Worse yet, Cleburne had pushed two regiments off Tunnel Hill and onto the flat near the Glass farm, opposite the left flank of the Ninetieth Illinois.

After thirty minutes in this untenable position, Loomis summoned two regiments to roust the Confederates from the farm. Lieutenant Colonel Joseph Taft of the Seventy-third Pennsylvania led his own regiment and the Twenty-seventh Pennsylvania across the flat on the run, sweeping the Rebels from the Glass farm. Taft ordered a halt at the foot of Tunnel Hill, but his order was misunderstood, and the Twenty-seventh Pennsylvania continued upward to within thirty yards of the hilltop.

Back on the flat, Loomis imagined that the Confederates were preparing to sally forth of Tunnel Hill into the gap that Taft had failed to close. Desperate to forestall an attack, Loomis again pleaded for

reinforcements. Again only a single brigade was sent to bolster the flagging Federal attack. This time the duty fell to Brigadier General Charles Matthies. Confederate artillery pulverized his brigade as it crossed the flat, and the survivors took cover along a sunken wagon road.

As his brigade sorted itself out, Matthies realized that he had veered too far to the left to cover Loomis's flank. In an effort to close the gap, he ordered the Tenth Iowa from the foot of Tunnel Hill over to the far right. Colonel Holden Putnam, the commander of the Ninety-third Illinois, led his regiment up the hill at full tilt. Putnam was shot dead and his Illinoisans were stopped thirty yards from the crest. Regrettably, General Matthies chose to reinforce what clearly was a losing proposition, sending all but the Fifth Iowa up to bolster the Ninety-third Illinois. Matthies went up himself a few minutes later, only to be struck by a bullet in the head. In the distance was another double line of blue sweeping across the flat, alone and unsupported. It was the brigade of Brigadier General Green Raum, whom Sherman committed to the stalled attack against Tunnel Hill at 2:00 P.M. By the time Raum reached Tunnel Hill, the

THE EAST TENNESSEE AND GEORGIA RAILROAD PASSES THROUGH MISSIONARY RIDGE AT TUNNEL HILL.

(LC)

situation along Matthies's front had deteriorated beyond repair. In hopes of reversing the tide, Raum sent two of his regiments up the hill.

Cleburne was in trouble. With Raum's two fresh regiments about to hit his front, Corse's Federals plunking away at his right flank, and the ammunition of his men down to only a handful of cartridges, it looked for the first time that afternoon as if Cleburne's salient might be broken.

But fortune favored the Irishman. General Hardee had plied Cleburne with reinforcements. With the advantage of interior lines and easy ground to traverse, the Rebels could marshal troops on and near Tunnel Hill far faster than Sherman's disorganized generals could bring units to bear against it. Cleburne fed fresh troops into the line just as Raum's two regiments charged past Matthies's stalled brigade. After Raum was halted, Cleburne ordered a counterattack all along the line.

The effect was electric. The Rebels bounded down the slope at 4:00 P.M. So spontaneous did the effort seem that some participants swore no order was ever given to charge.

After three nerve-wracking hours, the Federals had neither the strength nor the ammunition to resist. Yankees surrendered by the score, and the survivors slipped across the flat to safety. General John Smith was on hand to greet them, "smoking a pipe as calmly as he would in camp," reflected a begrimed survivor. "Well, boys, that's a tough place up there," he laughed. His joke fell flat, and the men drifted past in sullen silence.

So ended one of the sorriest episodes in this or any other battle of the war. In his assault on Tunnel Hill, Sherman exhibited an egregious lack of imagination. He attacked Cleburne's

salient head-on and with only a fraction of his force, rather than look for a way to outflank Tunnel Hill.

Seldom did the war witness a more anxious gathering of surly senior officers than Grant, Thomas, and their staffs atop Orchard Knob. Churned by fears that

Sherman had failed in his attack and that Hooker was fatally stalled along Chattanooga Creek, all present were absorbed in a tension more palpable than the shell fragments that rained on the knob.

By mid-afternoon, Grant had run out of ideas. After much debate, Grant gave Wood these orders: "If you and Sheridan advance your divisions to the foot of the ridge, and there halt, I think it will menace Bragg's forces so as to relieve Sherman." Wood agreed to try.

Preparations were made to assault the ridge. Corps commander Gordon Granger explained the details of the plan to Wood: "You and Sheridan are to advance your divisions, carry the intrench-

GENERALS GRANGER, GRANT, AND THOMAS (CENTER, ON RISE) ATOP ORCHARD KNOB OBSERVE THE ADVANCE OF THE ARMY OF THE CUMBERLAND. PAINTING BY THURE DE THULSTRUP.

(LC)

Thomas stood apart, watching their going with trepidation. To his way of thinking, Grant intended to sacrifice the Army of the Cumberland in a quixotic effort to salvage Sherman.

ments at the base of the ridge, if you can, and, if you succeed, halt there. The movement is to be made at once, so give your orders to your brigade commanders immediately, and the signal to advance will be the rapid, successive discharge of the six guns of the battery." Thomas stood apart, watching their going with trepidation. To his way of thinking, Grant intended to sacrifice the Army of the Cumberland in a quixotic effort to salvage Sherman.

The Confederate fortifications opposite Thomas's four divisions looked menacing enough. Arrayed along a front slightly less than three miles long were the better part of four Rebel divisions and nine batteries of artillery—approximately 16,000 men defending the seemingly impregnable heights against an attacking force of 23,000 that had nearly a mile of largely open ground to cross.

Imposing at first glance, the Confederate defenses were in reality a horribly improvised, sadly neglected patchwork. Their sorry state stemmed largely from the misplaced faith of both Bragg and Breckinridge that any serious attack would come only against the army's flanks.

The flaws in the Confederate defenses were numerous. Bragg and Breckinridge had waited until November 23 to begin fortifying the ridge. That night, Breckinridge ordered breastworks

built along the crest and Patton Anderson to supply the troops to construct them. With the apparent concurrence of Bragg, he issued a second order that took Anderson by surprise. He was to leave half of his division in the trenches at the foot of Missionary Ridge and withdraw the remainder to defend the crest. Zachariah Deas was to command the former troops, Anderson those atop the ridge.

Oddly, Breckinridge gave no such instructions to Bate or Stewart. He made no provision to withdraw any part of Bate's two brigades, then entrenched at the base, or to remove his artillery. Stewart also was left in the valley with his division.

Neither Anderson nor his brigade commanders Deas and Arthur Manigault cared for Breckinridge's plan; splitting the division between two lines struck them as the height of folly. Nor was the line chosen on the crest appropriate, being too far back to be of much use. There were too many undulations, projections, descents, and ravines to provide an adequate field of fire along the whole ridge.

For the artillery, the problem was even more acute. Not only were the cannon run too far forward, but they were too widely dispersed.

One final, potentially fatal flaw existed in Breckinridge's attenuated sector: he had no reserves with which to plug any

FEDERAL ENGINEERS
REBUILT THIS RAILROAD
BRIDGE AT WHITESIDE,
TENNESSEE, OUTSIDE
OF CHATTANOOGA
AFTER THE BATTLE.
CHATTANOOGA WOULD
SERVE AS AN IMPORTANT
BASE OF OPERATIONS
FOR FUTURE CAMPAIGNS
IN GEORGIA.

(LC)

hole that the Federals might punch into the narrow crest. Every man was committed, either to the rifle pits at the foot of Missionary Ridge or the breastworks atop it.

So matters stood until the morning of November 25, when Thomas pushed forward his skirmishers to test the strength of Deas's defenses. They were repulsed after a sharp fight, but their probe demonstrated that the Yankees might do what Bragg and Breckinridge found unimaginable: attack the center in force. The two still were unwilling to abandon the flat, but they struck a bizarre compromise with Brigadier General Zachariah Deas, who commanded part of the forces on the flat. Should the enemy advance in force, Deas's troops—and all others on the flat—were to hold their position until the Yankees approached to within 200 yards, then deliver a single volley and retire up the slope, skirmishing as they climbed. What such a tactic might accomplish, short of blocking the line of fire of those at the top and exhausting the men at the bottom, neither Bragg nor Breckinridge ventured to explain.

On the plain beyond Missionary Ridge, blue-clad troops by the thousands assembled. Rebel artillery from the crest boomed its greeting. As long as they were in the timber, the Federals knew they were fairly safe: the woods would provide at least a modicum of shelter for half the distance of their advance. But over the final 300 to 700 yards of the plain the Rebels had chopped down every last tree, both for firewood and to open a field of fire. From the rifle pits to the physical base of the ridge was a plateau about 100 yards wide, upon which the Confederates had built a cluster of huts.

Granger told his division commanders to deploy with all their brigades on line. Each brigade was to cover itself with a double line of skirmishers and maintain a strong reserve. All was ready by 3:00 P.M. Baird assembled on the left of Wood. Edward H. Phelps's brigade was arrayed on the extreme left of Baird's line, opposite Alfred Vaughan's brigade of Anderson's Rebel division. Ferdinand Van Derveer held Baird's center, and John Turchin formed his brigade on the right.

Wood deployed his division with Sam Beatty on the left, August Willich in the center, and William Hazen on the right of his division. Phil Sheridan had George Wagner, Charles Harker, and Francis Sherman lined up from left to right. Harker's command assembled a mile

THE BATTLE OF
MISSIONARY RIDGE,
NOVEMBER 25
*With the loss of
Lookout Mountain
on November 24 and
the appearance of
Sherman on the
Confederate right
flank, Bragg with-
drew his troops to
Missionary Ridge.*

*At mid-morning,
Sherman began a
series of attacks
against Confederates
under Cleburne sta-
tioned on Tunnel
Hill. Cleburne was
able to blunt each of
the Federal attacks,
preventing Sherman
from rolling up the
Confederate right.
Hooker began a suc-
cessful assault north-
ward from Rossville
Gap, driving in the
Confederate left.*

*Grant ordered
Thomas's Army of
the Cumberland to
seize the Confederate
rifle pits at the base
of Missionary Ridge.
Troops of Granger's
and Palmer's corps
swept forward, cap-
tured the rifle pits,
and then continued
up the slopes of
Missionary Ridge to
the crest. In so doing,
they broke the
Confederate line and
forced Bragg into a
withdrawal from the
Chattanooga area.*

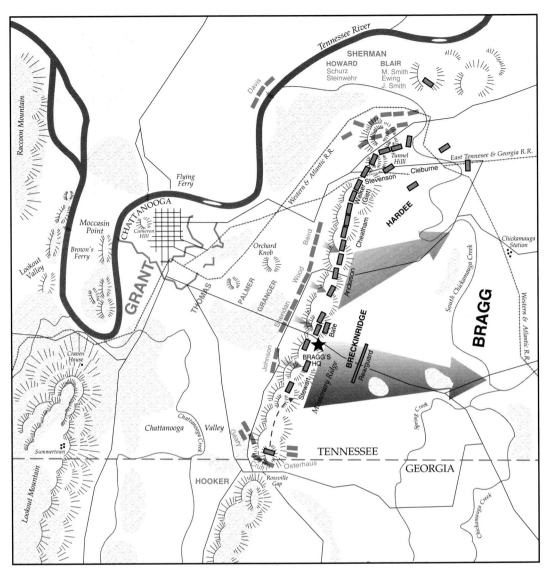

west of Bragg's headquarters.

On Granger's right, Palmer's Fourteenth Corps was represented solely by Richard Johnson's division. Johnson formed the brigades of William Stoughton and William Carlin in line of battle, leaving that of Starkweather behind to man the fortifications.

The men were formed quickly, but several senior officers in both the Fourth and Fourteenth corps were confused about what was expected of them. They were unsure how far they were supposed to advance or what to do when they got to where they were going. Grant's order to halt at the rifle pits at the base of the ridge was misunderstood by far too many of the generals charged with executing it. Some doubted the order because they

thought it absurd to stop an attack at the instant when the attackers would be most vulnerable both to fire from the crest and to a counterattack. Others apparently received garbled versions of the order.

Baird got the correct version; he simply couldn't believe it. So he decided to go for the summit. Wood said he received the correct order directly from Granger and that he then called together his brigade commanders to repeat it to them verbatim. But something went wrong. Hazen and every man in his brigade understood the task at hand. Sam Beatty may have understood the order as well, but his front-line regimental commanders were unsure where they were to stop. Willich swore that he only learned several days afterward that the order had been "to take only the rifle pits at the foot of the ridge."

Phil Sheridan was thoroughly befuddled. His confusion about the objective trickled down to his subordinates, who went forward blindly. And Richard Johnson had only a vague idea what was about to happen, which left his brigade commanders largely on their own. "My instructions were not very definite," said William Carlin. So he came up with his own. Riding along his line of battle, he shouted: "Boys, I don't want you to stop until we reach the top of that hill."

Twenty-three thousand officers and men lay in line of battle in Chattanooga Valley, waiting for the inevitable six-gun volley that would sound the march to whatever awaited them. It came at about 3:30 P.M. The first moments of the advance passed in silence. Then, through the branches of the naked trees, the Federals saw bright flames spew from the ridge and strands of dull gray smoke curl upward. An instant later, a crash like a thousand thunderclaps shook the valley. Attackers and defenders alike were deafened. None had ever heard such a cannonading in mountainous country before.

The air was sibilant with screaming shells, but the Confederate artillerymen overshot their targets. Some Yankee regiments lost not a man to the cannonade; most, fewer than a dozen. As the Federals emerged from the timber, they caught sight of the Rebel rifle pits. A grand, spontaneous cheer swept along the Union line. Just as spontaneously, the Yankees accelerated their pace from the quick time to the double-quick time. Some regiments burst into an uncontrolled run.

The Confederate withdrawal from the rifle pits was even more ragged than the Federal advance toward them. Some units withdrew after firing one volley; others stayed and fought it out until they were overrun; most ran as soon as they were able. When the survivors reached the crest, their presence wrought chaos. Their wild pushing and shoving as they tried to get to the rear frightened and demoralized their comrades on the crest. The Federals below were only slightly better off. Panting and

THIS SKETCH BY
THEODORE DAVIS
SHOWS THE WIDE
EXPANSE OF
MISSIONARY RIDGE AS
THE FOURTH CORPS
UNDER GRANGER
PREPARES ITS ADVANCE.

(LC)

coughing, they collapsed in the abandoned rifle pits.

Yankee skirmishers got to the rifle pits first. In about ten minutes the first-line regiments of each brigade joined them, creating a momentary jumble of bluecoats two miles long. Brigade commanders halted their subsequent lines out on the flat. They did so reluctantly, understanding that the Rebel artillery fire, until then ineffectual, would improve in accuracy with each minute their men lay in the open.

Meanwhile, the rifle pits themselves were proving death traps. As soon as the last of their comrades cleared their front, the Confederates on the crest sent volleys into the midst of the clustered Yankees. Then the greater portion of the Confederate artillery turned its attention from the flat to the rifle pits, changing their ammunition from shot and shell to canister.

In every mind there arose one thought: get out of the rifle pits immediately. For some commanders, of course, there really was no decision to be made; they incorrectly had understood Grant's order to be to seize the summit. For others, a continued advance at least to the

base of the ridge—from 200 to 400 yards away—seemed the only alternative to slaughter. There the contours of the slope would provide some cover from the rain of bullets, and its steepness would prevent the Rebel artillerymen from depressing their cannon tubes sufficiently to hit anyone.

In the first critical moments after taking the rifle pits, then, Thomas's four divisions moved independently of one another. Even brigades splintered as regimental commanders took the course of action that seemed most promising.

To August Willich went the honor of reaching the rifle pits first, a few minutes after 4:00 P.M. Willich had no intention of halting in them: "It was evident to everyone that to stay in this position would be certain destruction and final defeat; every soldier felt the necessity of saving the day and the campaign by conquering, and everyone saw instinctively that the only place of safety was in the enemy's works on the crest." Sam Beatty's brigade reached the rifle pits a few minutes after Willich. He too went up the slope full tilt. On the division right, Hazen also took his cue from Willich.

Sheridan was at least five minutes behind Wood in reaching the rifle pits. Wagner's brigade hit the pits a few moments before Harker and Sherman. The works were empty; the Rebels already were well on their way to the crest. In keeping with his assumption that Missionary Ridge was the objective, Wagner urged his men up the slope. Wagner's impetuous push inspired the regiments of Harker's brigade, and they also started upward. So too did Francis Sherman, but far more slowly, as his brigade faced a much steeper ascent. Cursing and swinging his sword, Sheridan rode along the edge of the rifle pits on a big black horse, slapping at skulkers.

Facing the steepest portion of the ridge, Richard Johnson's two brigades edged forward tentatively, preferring the cover of the Rebel huts on the plain to the uncertainties of the slope.

On the Union left, Baird too had run into trouble. The brigades of Phelps and Van Derveer reached and cleared the lower rifle pits ten minutes after Wood's division had done the same on their right. But Turchin's brigade was still hurrying across the flat, trying to catch up. Perhaps because Turchin was lagging behind,

Phelps and Van Derveer elected to halt their first line at the rifle pits. Both also directed their second-line regiments to lie down back on the flat. Fortunately, neither line suffered much. Vaughan's Tennesseans were retreating, masking their comrades on the crest, so that their fire at Phelps was erratic. And the artillery was "harmless but annoying."

Turchin had no intention of stopping at the rifle pits. His men reached them even more winded than their comrades to their left, but Turchin ordered them on; with or without support, he would obey Baird's order to seize the crest.

It was 4:10 P.M. when Turchin started up the ridge, just thirty minutes after the signal guns had barked. Baird, Wood, Sheridan, and Johnson all wrestled with their own worries, giving little thought to the problems of the others. The craggy texture of the slope saved hundreds of Federal lives by preventing the Confederates along the summit from getting a good aim at the ascending enemy. At the same time, it made a burlesque of unit integrity among the attackers. Regiments broke up, but "the men formed and fought under any commander who

was near and who was headed towards the enemy," said an Ohioan. "All regular formations were soon lost," agreed a Kansan. "Great masses of men, who had crowded together in the places easiest of ascent, were climbing the steep at intervals and vying in their efforts to be first."

At the head of each cluster of soldiers were regimental or national colors so that, instead of one long line, the Federal assault gave the appearance of a series of arrow-like sorties.

Breckinridge's generals could have recited a litany of woes. First, friendly troops continued to disrupt fields of fire, as scores of frightened Rebels were still struggling for the safety of the crest, many stumbling upward less than fifty yards ahead of the Yankees. Second, smoke blanketed the crest and settled in the ravines up which the Yankees were snaking. Third, those Rebels who did fire were badly overshooting their mark. Fear of hitting their own men, the blinding smoke, and a reluctance to expose themselves above the trenches caused many to squeeze off shot haphazardly. Finally, most of the batteries could no longer depress their cannon tubes to engage the Yankees. Exasperated cannoneers resorted

to hurling lighted shells down the slope.

Nearer came the Federals. Puffing and perspiring, crawling on hands and knees where the incline was too steep or rugged to walk, they dragged themselves upward. Color-bearers toppled by the dozen. The noise was terrific. "Orders could not be heard ten feet, so almost all orders of officers were given by the motion of the hand or sword," said an Ohio major. "Each soldier moved as his courage and endurance dictated."

Patton Anderson watched the approach of Wood's division with deep misgiving. He appreciated the difficulties faced by his thin line of riflemen in the entrenchments. "Owing to the confirmation of the ridge, from which several spurs projected along my front, affording cover to the attacking forces, and protecting them from any but a direct fire . . . he was enabled to advance to within a short distance of the crest with relative impunity," rued the Floridian.

It was a few minutes before 5:00 P.M. Amid the lengthening shadows, fifty yards away from the Rebel line, a small band of Willich's and Hazen's men rushed forward from behind an embankment along the Bird's Mill road. Over the log breastworks

Nearer came the Federals. Puffing and perspiring, crawling on hands and knees where the incline was too steep or rugged to walk, they dragged themselves upward.

A HIGHLY DRAMATIC RENDITION BY CURRIER AND IVES OF THE INTENSE HAND-TO-HAND COMBAT ON THE TOP OF THE RIDGE.

(LC)

they leaped before the startled Mississippians of Colonel William Tucker could fire a shot. Panic gripped the Rebels. They ran from the works by the score. Nearly as many surrendered.

Toward the breastworks clambered the remainder of Willich's brigade. Crowding Willich's left, having scurried for the shelter of a deep ravine, was Beatty's brigade, compacted to a front nearly as small as that of a normal-sized regiment.

For an instant, the issue hung in doubt. Sixty feet short of the entrenchments, the Federals wavered—stopped by a fierce Rebel volley and their own fatigue. The arrival of Beatty's reserve restored the momentum of the attack, and the Yankees made a last dash for the breastworks. In a moment they were over, grappling briefly with Tucker's Mississippians before the mad panic that had struck Tucker's left center infected his entire line.

A few hundred feet down the ridge, the rest of Hazen's brigade came up. A fortuitous undulation in the slope helped shelter Hazen's men until they were just three yards from the breastworks. By then the Rebels had fired their final volley and had no time to reload. Over the logs climbed the Federals. "We were up the hill in a very few moments, and some of the Rebels who had been murdering our men to the last moment, rolled over on their backs and looked up in a very pitiful attitude," said Colonel James Foy, who was leading the charge.

Bragg was near Bate. The sudden appearance of Foy's Yankees left him dumbstruck; he had been congratulating Bate's men for having sent the brigades of Wagner and Harker recoiling down the ridge. Now he felt the absence of a tactical reserve. He implored Bate to spare whatever troops he could from his own breastworks to drive away the Federals and restore the break on Anderson's front.

Bate felt mortified but unable to

respond. Wagner and Harker were on the move again and almost halfway up the ridge to his front, "advancing in such numbers as to forbid the displacement of any of my command."

Hazen was on the crest now, driving his reformed brigade relentlessly southward. Colonel Tyler tried to pull back his right-flank units to meet Hazen, but a bullet cut him down before he could fashion an adequate firing line. Hazen's Yankees made short work of Tyler's leaderless brigade. "The Federals [ran] over us like a herd of wild cattle," confessed one frightened Tennessean.

Wagner's brigade crowned the crest a few minutes later. No brigade suffered more in ascending Missionary Ridge than did Wagner's. He lost 730 men: three times more than did Sam Beatty and more than twice the casualties sustained by the brigades of Francis Sherman, Harker, or Willich. Only Hazen's losses of 522 came close.

Having suffered so much, the disappointment of Wagner and his troops at finding the crest virtually abandoned was almost unbearable. Everyone had wanted a chance to sink his bayonet into a Rebel.

On Wagner's right, Charles Harker

and his brigade enjoyed a more stirring climax to their ninety-minute ordeal. They swarmed over the summit a minute or two before Wagner reached the crest to find the Rebel infantry had retreated. But while Harker's Federals were denied the chance to cross bayonets with the enemy, they found compensation awaiting them beyond the breastworks. There, on the narrow crest beside Bragg's headquarters, struggling to bring off their four Napoleon twelve-pounders, were the Kentuckians of Cobb's Battery. As the Federals surged toward them, most of the gunners prudently ran off. The rest gave up or were cut down.

Bragg had been shuttling along the ridge, trying with almost comic desperation to rally first Tucker's broken brigade, then Finley's Floridians, and finally Gibson's Louisiana Brigade, which crumbled before Francis Sherman's Federals. Near the front yard of the Moore house, Bragg sat astride his horse holding a large flag, imploring men who detested the sight of him to hold their ground.

With nothing but blue to be seen on the crest, Bragg remounted and turned his

horse rearward to join the retreating throng. In any meaningful sense, the center of his supposedly impregnable Missionary Ridge line had ceased to exist.

But there was still killing and running aplenty going on along the doomed sector. Francis Sherman had managed to get his men out of the rifle pits at the foot of the ridge and on their way toward a lightly defended second line partway up that was defended by elements of Strahl's Tennessee brigade. Once they got started, Sherman's men had no trouble rolling over the Tennesseans.

Sherman gave his men ten minutes to recover their strength. Then, with a rush, they swarmed out of the second trench. The Rebels fought like fiends for as long as they could, but here too the terrain betrayed the defenders. The same sharp incline that winded the Yankees also kept the Rebels from getting a clear shot without showing themselves above their low works. So, instead, they lay down and hurled rocks and lighted shells randomly downhill.

Over the top came the Federals. The Rebel infantry ran off, taunted by the same cries of "Chickamauga, Chickamauga!" they had been hurling at their foe. Throughout Sherman's brigade, exhaustion gave way to ecstasy as the men crowded around four guns of a Rebel battery abandoned in the melee.

Sherman's appearance on the crest, although as dramatic as that of any other brigade, was anticlimactic insofar as the defeat of Bate was concerned. But it did

make an important contribution to dislodging Stewart, whose division at 5:15 P.M. was the only Confederate force left on the ridge south of Bragg's headquarters.

Stewart was holding on because Richard Johnson's two brigades were making no headway against the thread of a line held by Strahl's left regiments and Stovall's brigades. Stoughton's mixed brigade of regulars and volunteers was repulsed in its first effort at clearing out

the Tennesseans from the rifle pits on the slope. By the time Stoughton took them, Sherman's men were going over the top. Stoughton rested his men, then drove hard to make up the lost ground. His effort halted abruptly. Though Strahl's troops on the crest were putting up a gallant resistance, their numbers alone were too few to stop the Yankees; what caused Stoughton to lag behind was the almost perpendicular wall formed by the ridge over the last two hundred feet of his front. Stoughton might have languished on the dizzying incline longer had Sherman's success on his left not compelled Strahl

A SENTRY GUARDS CAPTURED CONFEDERATE GUNS AFTER THE BATTLE.

(LC)

finally to give up his line along the crest.

Brigadier General William Carlin confessed: "I started up the ridge because I saw the troops on my left going up, but who gave the original impulse it would be hard to ascertain." Carlin had made the only choice possible, but his decision was irrelevant: the men already had taken matters into their own hands. "They were like a headstrong horse with a bit in his teeth, beyond holding in," said Carlin's second-in-command, Benjamin Scribner. Carlin's brigade carried their portion of the crest at 5:30 P.M., at the cost of more perspiration than blood; Stewart had ordered Stovall to withdraw before the Yankees reached the top.

Matters were desperate on the Confederate left, where General Breckinridge had gone at 3:30 P.M. When he arrived, Colonel J. T. Holtzclaw was watching the approach of Fighting Joe Hooker's powerful Federal column from the direction of Lookout Mountain. As the Yankees crossed Chattanooga Creek and made for the undefended Rossville Gap, the key to the Confederate left flank, Breckinridge realized he would have to fend off Hooker's three divisions with Holtzclaw's five understrength Alabama regiments.

The Yankees marched through Rossville Gap, brushing aside the handful of Rebels who had been guarding the supplies and wagons at Rossville, before Breckinridge could send more troops to oppose them. Once through, the Federals

regrouped for a go at the ridge itself. Hooker improvised a scheme of maneuver. He told Cruft to swing north, get onto Missionary Ridge, and then "engage the enemy vigorously in case he should be met, pressing the line rapidly northward along the ridge until the enemy was encountered." To John Geary, who was closing on Rossville, he gave orders to leave the road short of the gap and march northward along the western base of the ridge.

It was a brilliant plan, the more so for its simplicity. Cruft would take the Confederates in the flank; Geary would feel for a chance to strike a weak point from in front; and Osterhaus would net from behind any Rebels trying to flee the field.

The execution was as sound as the conception. Holtzclaw's brigade was boxed in between Hooker's three divisions and Carlin's brigade of Johnson's division. Finding Federals on all four sides, nearly all the Confederates gave up; Carlin's troops alone netted 706 officers and men.

The Federal assault on Anderson's division followed a discernible pattern. Anderson's brigades folded from south to north, as Union forces pushed them from in front and rolled up their flank. Regiments of Willich's and Beatty's brigade, after clearing Tucker's Mississippians from their front, turned captured cannon on the enemy and swept northward. Their pressure on Manigault's left flank hastened his collapse. All of these events—from the rout of Tucker to the defeat of Manigault—lasted no more than fifteen or twenty minutes.

Just as it did Manigault, the unexpected pressure on Deas's flank doomed the Alabamian. He withdrew his left regiments before the Yankees in front of them reached the crest but was too late to save either his right regiments or three of the four guns of Waters's battery.

Van Derveer joined Turchin, and together their badly intermingled brigades headed toward the last of Anderson's brigades: the four Tennessee regiments of Brigadier General Alfred Vaughan. At Anderson's behest, he peeled off two of his regiments from the breastworks in a hopeless effort at stemming Van Derveer and Turchin. The two lines blazed away at a hundred yards until the Tennesseans ran out of ammunition. Vaughan conceded the contest, retreating by the left flank off Missionary Ridge.

Vaughan's withdrawal ended the battle for the Confederate center and right. As twilight deepened into a purple and gunsmoke gray darkness, every unit of Anderson's, Bate's, and Stewart's divisions was either tentatively reforming among the foothills east of Missionary Ridge or else in headlong retreat toward Chickamauga Station. Only Cheatham's and Cleburne's divisions of Hardee's right wing remained of what Bragg and Breckinridge had deemed to be an impregnable line. Frank Cheatham was fully cognizant of the disaster unfolding to his left. Shortly after the Federals started across the valley, Cheatham had surmised that few if any of the attackers would strike his portion of the line on Missionary Ridge. Consequently, he rode to the extreme left of his division to watch the fight unfold on Anderson's front. The Tennessean sat behind Jackson's brigade. To Jackson's right were the decimated commands of Walthall and Moore. The moment Vaughan began to flounder, Cheatham ordered Jackson and Moore to change front to the left. Only McCants's Florida Battery stayed put to hold the line against Phelps's left regiments, which, contrary to Cheatham's calculations, were climbing the ridge in front of Jackson.

In the fast-fading light, Jackson and Moore were able to stop Van Derveer's advance northward along the crest. But Baird and Van Derveer had reserves to feed into the fight, and after thirty minutes in action, Jackson's brigade fled. With his flank exposed, Moore withdrew as well. Most of Phelps's brigade was on Missionary Ridge now, and his and Van

As twilight deepened into a purple and gunsmoke gray darkness, every unit of Anderson's, Bate's, and Stewart's divisions was either tentatively reforming among the foothills east of Missionary Ridge or else in headlong retreat . . .

Derveer's men surged northward.

Cheatham scrambled to place another obstacle before their further progress. Baird was just one mile from Tunnel Hill. All Cheatham had left to stop—or at least slow—him was Walthall's fragment of a brigade, which he now brought into play. Walthall's Mississippians, few though they were, proved sufficient for the task at hand. A few volleys halted the Yankees, who came no nearer than 200 yards, and after several more minutes of frenetic shooting by both sides, they

ceased fire and backed out of range. It was about 6:00 P.M.

Darkness, more than the Mississippians, had put an end to Baird's advance. And, despite their superior numbers, the Yankees were disorganized and exhausted. All seemed content to let the Confederates leave the field at their leisure. The fight for Missionary Ridge was over.

The night of November 25, 1863, was the saddest to date in the depressing history of the Army of Tennessee. Over three rough country lanes, the heartbroken troops of Bragg's dispersed divisions moved toward South Chickamauga Creek, on the far bank of which they might find at lest temporary safety. Awaiting them at Chickamauga Station was Bragg, as distraught as his men.

Bragg understood that the army's stay at Chickamauga Station must be brief, as the Federals were likely to pursue before dawn. Planning to leave shortly after midnight, Bragg chose as the immediate objective of his retreat Ringgold, Georgia, a town ten miles southeast of Chickamauga Station astride the strategically vital Western and Atlantic Railroad. Just beyond Ringgold, the railroad passed through a gap in a thirty-mile-long ridge known as Taylor's Ridge south of the tracks and White Oak Mountain north of them. From Ringgold, Bragg planned to retire fifteen miles farther to Dalton.

Where were the Yankees during the long, cold night of November 25? Why did no columns of jubilant bluecoats come bursting through the dark forest west of South Chickamauga Creek to consume the weary Rebels?

The answer rested with Grant. Having won a stunning though unexpected victory on Missionary Ridge, he was momentarily at a loss what to do next. And the last Confederates scarcely had disappeared from Missionary Ridge before Grant felt obliged to turn the better part of his attention to a problem more vexing than finishing off Bragg: what to do about General Burnside, who reportedly was besieged at Knoxville by Longstreet and low on provisions. The pressure from Washington to help Burnside and his uncertainty over affairs on his own front rendered Grant unable to fashion a fast, coordinated pursuit of Bragg during the night of November 25. Instead, he fashioned a compromise strategy. At daylight, he would chase Bragg with Sherman's troops and part of Thomas's army; Granger, meanwhile, would take his corps to succor Burnside.

The pursuit got off to a rocky start, and Bragg's infantry passed through Ringgold intact before nightfall on the twenty-sixth. It ground completely to a halt the next day, when Pat Cleburne, commanding the rear guard, successfully defended Ringgold Gap against a series of poorly orchestrated attacks by Fighting Joe Hooker. Although outnumbered three to one, Cleburne had deployed his division along White Oak Mountain and Taylor's Ridge so as to avail himself of the advantages the high ground offered. He held on until noon, when word came that the army trains were safely on their way to Dalton and that he might withdraw as he pleased. In saving the trains and artillery of the Army of Tennessee, Cleburne had lost 221 men, while inflicting over 500 casualties.

Ringgold Gap marked the end of the Chattanooga campaign, the most decisive to date in the West. Bragg had lost a campaign; a week later, he lost his command. President Davis at last conceded the need to relieve him. But a change in commanders could not mask the fact that the South had been dealt a devastating blow. Counting those of Cleburne's division who fell at Ringgold Gap, the Army of Tennessee reported casualties of 6,667 in the battles for Chattanooga; that is, Orchard Knob, Lookout Mountain, and Missionary Ridge. Of these, 4,146 were counted as missing. Grant, however,

insisted that he sent 6,142 men to Union prison camps. His count probably is more reliable, reflecting the hundreds of stragglers netted during the pursuit from Chickamauga Station to Ringgold Gap. Equally serious was the loss in artillery. Forty cannon and 69 limbers and caissons had been surrendered or abandoned, most on Missionary Ridge.

By comparison, Grant had suffered 686 killed, 4,329 wounded, and just 322 captured or missing. Sheridan's division had sustained nearly a quarter of these casualties: 1,346, almost all in the assault on Missionary Ridge.

Although volunteers were virtually nonexistent in the Confederacy and able-bodied conscripts as scarce as hard currency, it was still easier to replace men than to regain territory. The South had lost for good the state of Tennessee. The late autumn offensive of John B. Hood's

ragged and sick remnant of an army a year later could not change that reality. From November 26, 1863, until the end of the war, the South would be on the strategic defensive in the West.

Of course, the South's loss was the North's gain. Union armies now had secure lines of communication from the Ohio River to Chattanooga. The city became a giant storehouse, where supplies stockpiled during the winter months made possible Sherman's spring 1864 offensive against the last virgin reaches of the Confederate heartland—the interior of Georgia.

The Chattanooga campaign also cemented the triumvirate that would win the war: Grant, Sherman, and Sheridan. Grant's star, which had faded briefly after Vicksburg, was to burn brightly from then on, illuminating a path to the White House.

The Chattanooga campaign also cemented the triumvirate that would win the war: Grant, Sherman, and Sheridan.

GENERAL GRANT (LEFT) RELAXES ON LOOKOUT MOUNTAIN AFTER THE VICTORY AT CHATTANOOGA.

(LC)